From Seed to Sustenance:

The Ultimate Scripture for Preserving Biodiversity, Nurturing Garden Abundance, and Ensuring Food Sovereignty through Seed Saving

John E. Sain

Copyright © 2023

All rights reserved. No part of this publication may be reproduced, distributed, or transmitted in any form or by any means, including photocopying, recording, or other electronic or mechanical methods, without the prior written permission of the publisher, except in the case of brief quotations embodied in critical reviews and certain other noncommercial uses permitted by copyright law.

The information contained in this book is intended for educational purposes only and is not intended to replace the advice of a professional. The author and publisher have made every effort to ensure the accuracy of the information herein. However, the author and publisher make no representation or warranties with respect to the accuracy or completeness of the contents of this book and specifically disclaim any implied warranties of merchantability or fitness for a particular purpose. The information contained herein is provided on an "as is" basis without warranty of any kind.

The author and publisher shall have no liability or responsibility to any person or entity with respect to any loss or damage caused, or alleged to be caused, directly or indirectly by the information contained in this book.

Trademarks, service marks, and logos appearing in this book are the property of their respective owners. They are used for identification purposes only and not for endorsement, sponsorship, or affiliation.

Summary

Chapter 1: Seed Saving Overview

Seed saving is a process of preserving and cultivating plant seeds to grow and reproduce plants in a sustainable manner. It is a time-honored tradition passed down from generation to generation, with the earliest known evidence of seed saving dating back to over 12,000 years ago. The practice has been an integral part of agriculture, ensuring a continuous supply of food to nourish human populations. In modern times, seed saving has become increasingly important, particularly with the rise of industrial agriculture. This chapter will provide an overview of seed saving, including its history, benefits, and techniques.

History of Seed Saving

Seed saving has played a critical role in human civilization. It allowed ancient civilizations to develop agricultural practices that fed their populations and enabled their societies to thrive. Farmers saved seeds from their best-performing crops and planted them the following year, effectively selecting for desirable traits and developing new species and varieties over time. Through this process, farmers developed crops with improved resistance to pests, greater yields, and superior nutritional content.

As agriculture became more industrialized, the practice of seed saving began to decline. Large agricultural corporations gradually took control of seed production and distribution, effectively monopolizing the market and limiting the availability of traditional varieties. The market became increasingly focused on high-yielding, hybridized seeds that required the use of chemical fertilizers and pesticides to achieve optimal crop production.

This shift to industrial agriculture created a dependence on high-cost inputs and left farmers vulnerable to declining crop yields and environmental degradation. Seed saving became more important than ever as a way to ensure biodiversity and sustainable farming practices. It allowed farmers to control their own seed production and develop new varieties adapted to local conditions, resulting in greater food security and economic independence.

Benefits of Seed Saving

Seed saving has numerous benefits for both farmers and the environment. Here are some of the key benefits:

1. Biodiversity: Saving seeds of traditional or heirloom varieties can help preserve genetic diversity and prevent the loss of unique plant traits.

2. Adaptability: Plants grown from saved seeds are well adapted to local conditions, including soil type, climate, pests, and diseases.

3. Food security: Saving seeds enables farmers to control their own seed supply, ensuring a continuous source of food even in times of

crop failure or market fluctuations.

4. Economic independence: By saving seeds, farmers can reduce their dependence on expensive patented seeds and chemical inputs, leading to greater economic independence.

5. Environmental protection: Using saved seeds promotes sustainable farming practices, reducing the use of chemical fertilizers, pesticides, and genetically modified organisms (GMOs).

Types of Seed Saving

There are several types of seed saving techniques, depending on the type of plant and seed. Here are the main types:

1. Self-pollinated plants: Self-pollinating plants are those that have flowers that contain both male and female reproductive organs. These plants can be saved by collecting the seed heads or pods once they are dry and mature. Examples of self-pollinating plants include beans, peas, tomatoes, lettuce, and peppers.

2. Cross-pollinated plants: Cross-pollinated plants are those that require pollen from another plant to fertilize their flowers. These plants require some intervention to ensure that they cross-pollinate properly. The most common method is to isolate plants by wrapping them in row covers or using hand-pollination techniques. Examples of cross-pollinated plants include squash, cucumbers, melons, and

corn.

3. Biennial plants: Biennial plants have a two-year life cycle, with the first year devoted to vegetative growth and the second year to flowering and seed production. These plants require extra attention to ensure that they do not die off during the winter, although some may be able to produce seed in their first year. Examples of biennial plants include carrots, beets, and onions.

Seed Storage

Proper seed storage is critical to ensure the viability of the seeds and maintain their genetic integrity over time. Here are some key tips to follow:

1. Drying: Seeds must be thoroughly dried before storage to prevent mold or fungal growth. Spread the seeds over a clean, dry surface in a warm, dry place for several days until they are completely dry.

2. Containers: Store seeds in airtight containers, such as glass jars or plastic bags. Be sure to label the container with the plant variety, date harvested, and any other pertinent information.

3. Location: Store seeds in a cool, dark, and dry location, such as a refrigerator or freezer. This will help to maintain seed viability over several years.

Seed saving is a time-honored tradition that has played a critical role in human civilization. It allows farmers to maintain biodiversity, adapt to local conditions, and promote sustainability in agriculture. With the rise of industrial agriculture, seed saving has become more important than ever as a way to ensure food security, economic independence, and the preservation of unique plant traits. By following proper seed saving and storage techniques, farmers can maintain a continuous supply of high-quality, traditional varieties of plants for generations to come.

Chapter 2: Importance of Seed Saving

Seed saving is the practice of collecting, storing, and replanting seeds from plants in order to preserve genetic diversity, ensure food security, and maintain agricultural sustainability. It is an essential and time-honored tradition that has been practiced by farmers, gardeners, and indigenous communities for centuries. The importance of seed saving can be understood through several key factors:

Genetic Diversity: Seeds are the carriers of genetic information that determines the characteristics and traits of plants. By saving and preserving a wide variety of seeds, we protect genetic diversity within plant populations. This diversity is crucial for plant resilience, adaptation to changing environmental conditions, and the development of new crop varieties. Preserving diverse seeds helps to safeguard against the loss of genetic resources, ensuring the availability of resilient plants for future generations.

Food Security and Sovereignty: In a world where global food systems heavily rely on a few commercial crop varieties, seed saving plays a vital role in ensuring food security and sovereignty. By saving seeds from locally adapted and traditional crop varieties, communities can maintain access to nutritious food sources, cultivate plants that are well-suited to their specific climates and growing conditions, and reduce dependence on external seed suppliers. Seed saving empowers farmers and gardeners to control their own seed supply, preserving traditional knowledge and promoting self-reliance in food production.

Adaptation to Climate Change: Climate change poses significant challenges to agricultural systems, with rising temperatures, changing rainfall patterns, and increased pest pressures. Saving seeds allows farmers and gardeners to select and replant seeds from plants that have demonstrated resilience and adaptability to local conditions. By saving seeds from plants that exhibit desirable traits such as drought tolerance, disease resistance, or heat resilience, communities can adapt their crops to changing climates and increase their chances of agricultural success.

Cultural Heritage and Traditional Knowledge: Seed saving is deeply rooted in cultural heritage and traditional knowledge. Many indigenous communities and farming cultures have developed intricate knowledge and practices around seed saving, passing down this wisdom from generation to generation. By preserving and continuing the practice of seed saving, we honor and value the diverse cultural traditions associated with agriculture and recognize the importance of indigenous knowledge systems in sustainable food production.

Biodiversity Conservation: Saving seeds contributes to the conservation of biodiversity by preserving unique and rare plant species. In addition to cultivated crop varieties, seed banks and seed-saving initiatives also focus on collecting and conserving wild and endangered plant species. This conservation effort helps protect ecosystems, supports the survival of threatened plants, and maintains a reservoir of genetic resources that can potentially be utilized for future scientific research, crop improvement, and ecological restoration.

In summary, seed saving is a crucial practice for maintaining genetic diversity, promoting food security and sovereignty, adapting to climate change, preserving cultural heritage, and conserving biodiversity. By actively participating in seed saving, individuals and communities play an important role in ensuring a sustainable and resilient future for agriculture and the environment.

Chapter 3: Historical Perspective of Seed Saving

Seed saving has been an essential practice in human civilization since the beginning of agriculture. The ability to save seeds and propagate them has allowed humans to have a sustainable food source, thus allowing for the development of civilizations. From ancient times, farmers have known the importance of selecting plants with desirable traits and saving their seeds to cultivate them again next season. This chapter looks at the historical perspective of seed saving, the methods used in ancient times, and how the industrialization of agriculture has changed this practice.

The History of Seed Saving:

Seed saving has been an essential part of agriculture for over 10,000 years. The ancient civilizations of the Fertile Crescent, including the Sumerians, Babylonians, and Assyrians, were some of the first to practice agriculture. These civilizations were responsible for creating the first agricultural systems, which included the cultivation of crops such as barley, wheat, and rye. The farmers of these civilizations used selective breeding to develop crops with desirable traits, such as disease resistance, higher yields, and better flavor. They would save the seeds from their best plants to plant next season and improve the quality of their crops.

Seed saving continued throughout the centuries, and by the middle ages, it had become a common practice among farmers. Farmers saved seeds from their best crops and traded them with other farmers for different varieties. Seed saving was vital during this time as crop failures were common, and the ability to plant seeds from the previous year's harvest provided a sustainable food source.

In the 17th century, the scientific revolution brought new methods of agriculture. Farmers began experimenting with crossbreeding to develop new crop varieties. John Woodward was one of the first scientists to publish experimental research on plants. He discovered that plants of the same species produced different offspring when crossed with other plants. This discovery led to the development of new crop varieties, which increased crop yields and improved resistance to disease.

During the 18th and 19th centuries, seed saving became more organized as seed companies emerged. Seed companies began offering mail-order catalogs, allowing farmers to order specific seeds for their crops. This made it easier for farmers to access a wide variety of seeds and create more diverse agricultural systems.

In the 20th century, agriculture saw a major shift as industrialization led to the development of new technologies to increase crop yields, such as chemical fertilizers and hybrid seeds. These new technologies made it possible for farmers to produce larger quantities of crops, more efficiently, and in less time. However, the increase in the use of hybrid seeds, which do not produce viable seeds, resulted in the decline in seed saving, as farmers were forced to purchase new seeds every season.

The Importance of Seed Saving:

Seed saving is essential for maintaining genetic diversity in crops. Genetic diversity is critical in breeding plants that can resist diseases and adapt to changing environmental conditions. Additionally, seed saving helps to preserve heirloom varieties that are unique to certain regions. These varieties are often grown by small-scale farmers and are not available through seed companies.

Seed saving also helps to reduce the dependence on hybrid and genetically modified seeds, which require farmers to purchase new seeds every season. By growing and saving their seeds, farmers can reduce their costs, maintain their independence, and preserve local knowledge of their unique seed varieties. Additionally, seed saving promotes sustainable agriculture and helps to protect the environment by reducing the use of chemical fertilizers and pesticides.

The Future of Seed Saving:

Today, seed saving is experiencing a resurgence as farmers and gardeners are becoming more interested in traditional methods of agriculture and working to preserve heirloom varieties. The rise of the organic and local food movements has led to increasing demand for sustainably grown food, which has resulted in more farmers returning to traditional methods of agriculture, including seed saving.

Additionally, the internet has made it easier for farmers to share knowledge and exchange seeds. Websites, such as Seed Savers Exchange, offer an online database of open-pollinated and heirloom seeds, and also facilitate seed exchanges between farmers.

Seed saving has been an essential practice in agriculture for over 10,000 years and has played a crucial role in the development of human civilization. The ability to save, trade, and cultivate seeds has allowed farmers to maintain a sustainable food source, improve crop yields, and preserve genetic diversity. Although the industrialization of agriculture has led to the decline of seed saving, the practice is experiencing a resurgence, as farmers and gardeners rediscover the importance of traditional methods of agriculture for sustainable food production.

Chapter 4: Seed Life Cycle

Have you ever wondered how a tiny seed can transform into a towering tree or a lush garden? The answer lies in the seed's life cycle – a fascinating process that encompasses all the stages of a plant's growth, from the moment the seed is planted to the point of reproducing new seeds.

In this chapter, we will delve into the intricacies of the seed life cycle, exploring each stage in detail, and understanding the underlying biological processes that govern them. So let's get started!

Seed Formation

The seed life cycle begins with the formation of a seed. A seed is the reproductive structure of a flowering plant that contains the embryo of the plant within it. It is formed after the pollination of the flower, which is when the male pollen grains fuse with the female ovules within the flower.

Once the ovules are fertilized, they develop into seeds, and the ovary of the flower develops into a fruit that encloses the seeds. The structure of the seed varies depending on the type of plant, but most seeds have three essential parts – the embryo, the endosperm, and the seed coat.

The embryo is the tiny plant enclosed within the seed, and it contains the cotyledons or embryonic leaves, the shoot tip, and the root tip. The endosperm is the food source for the developing embryo, and it provides the necessary nutrients for the seed to germinate.

The seed coat is the protective outer layer that encases the embryo and endosperm, and it helps to keep the seed viable and protected from external factors such as insects, diseases, and adverse environmental conditions.

Seed Dormancy

Once the seed is formed, it enters a state of dormancy, which is a period of inactivity or quiescence. Dormancy is a survival mechanism that allows the seed to remain inactive until favorable conditions for germination are present.

During dormancy, the metabolic activity of the seed slows down, and the seed coat becomes impermeable to water and oxygen. These factors ensure that the seed remains viable and protected for an extended period, sometimes for several years.

Dormancy can be broken by various environmental factors such as temperature, light, moisture, fire, or mechanical disturbance. These factors trigger physiological changes in the seed that enable it to overcome dormancy and begin germination.

Seed Germination

The next stage in the seed life cycle is germination, which is the process of the seed sprouting and developing into a seedling. Germination begins when the seed absorbs water and swells, leading to the rupture of the seed coat.

Once the seed coat is ruptured, the embryo begins to grow, and the root tip emerges first, followed by the shoot tip. The root system grows downward, anchoring the seedling into the soil, while the shoot system grows upward, seeking light and air.

During this phase, the endosperm acts as the primary source of energy for the developing seedling until the cotyledons emerge and begin producing food through photosynthesis.

Seedling Development

As the seedlings grow, they develop their true leaves and start to resemble the adult plant. At this stage, the seedling is still vulnerable and requires the right conditions for healthy growth.

Factors such as light, temperature, moisture, and nutrients are crucial for seedling development, and any deficiencies can stunt growth or even lead to death.

As the seedling grows, its root system becomes more extensive, allowing it to absorb water and nutrients from the soil. The shoot system also becomes more complex, producing branches, leaves, and flowers, depending on the plant's species.

Reproductive Stage

The final stage in the seed life cycle is the reproductive stage, where the adult plant produces flowers and new seeds. The reproductive process begins when the plant's flowers are pollinated, and the ovules within the flower are fertilized.

After fertilization, the ovules develop into new seeds, and the fruit of the plant helps to disperse the seeds, ensuring the plant's survival.

The seed life cycle is a fascinating and complex process that underpins the growth and survival of all flowering plants. From the formation of the seed to the production of new seeds, every stage is vital for the plant's growth and survival.

Understanding the seed life cycle can help us to become better gardeners and farmers, as well as appreciate the beauty and complexity of the natural world. So next time you see a tiny seed, remember that it contains the potential for an entire life cycle, waiting to unfold.

Chapter 5: Seed Harvesting Techniques

Seed harvesting techniques refer to the methods used to store, collect and prepare seeds for planting. Seeds are essential for plant growth, multiplication, and regeneration. Harvesting seeds is crucial in maintaining the genetic diversity of plant species. It also helps to conserve rare and endangered plants. There are several seed harvesting techniques that one can use to ensure the viability of the seeds. This chapter provides an in-depth insight into some of the most common seed harvesting techniques.

1. Manual seed harvesting

Manual seed harvesting is one of the oldest and simplest seed harvesting techniques. It involves the use of hands to collect seeds from mature plants. The plants are left to dry on the stalks after their flowering season before harvesting. The seeds are then stripped from the plants and stored in a cool, dry place to prevent them from rotting or molding.

Manual seed harvesting is useful for plants that do not produce large quantities of seeds, such as flowers. However, it can be time-consuming and labor-intensive, making it unsuitable for commercial scale seed harvesting.

2. Machine seed harvesting

Machine seed harvesting involves the use of specialized equipment to collect seeds in large quantities. The equipment includes seed harvester, threshers and combines. Seed harvesters can harvest seeds from different types of crops, including soybeans, corn or sunflowers. The machines are designed to shake the seeds off the plants and then separate them from the chaff.

Machine seed harvesting is faster and more efficient than manual harvesting, making it suitable for large-scale commercial seed production. However, it is expensive to operate, and the machines can damage the seeds or reduce their viability.

3. Seed stripping

Seed stripping is a technique used by some plants to shed their seeds by force. Some plants have unique structures called "strawberry runners" that collect the seed automatically. Examples of such plants include strawberries, blackberries, raspberries, and brambles. The technique involves waiting for the plant to produce mature fruit. Once the fruit is mature, it drops the seeds, which are then collected.

Seed stripping is useful for plants that produce a moderate number of seeds like berries. However, it is not suitable for plants that produce large numbers of seed like rice or corn.

4. Seed beating

Seed beating is a technique that involves beating sacks of harvested plants to force the seeds out of the heads. The plants are hung upside down in a large bag, and the seeds are then beaten out using sticks or other similar tools. Seed beating is useful for crops that produce hard-to-remove seeds, like sunflowers.

Seed beating is time-consuming and labor-intensive, making it unsuitable for large-scale seed production. It is also not very effective in removing all the seeds from the crop.

5. Dry casting

Dry casting is a seed sowing technique that involves scattering the seeds over a prepared area of ground. The technique is useful for crops that produce a large number of seeds, such as wildflowers. Dry casting is beneficial as the seeds fall where they will have the best chances of germinating and growing into mature plants.

Dry casting is simple, inexpensive, and requires minimal machinery, making it suitable for small-scale planting. It is unsuitable for crops that require high density planting, such as wheat or rice fields.

6. Wet casting

Wet casting is a seed sowing technique that involves soaking the seeds in water before scattering them over a prepared area of land. The technique is useful for crops that require a moist environment to germinate and grow, such as some types of trees. Wet casting helps to ensure that the seeds absorb water, making them more likely to germinate.

Wet casting is suitable for planting in wetland environments, but it is unsuitable for planting on dry lands. The technique can also lead to the loss of valuable seeds if the seeds are not sown correctly.

7. Direct seeding

Direct seeding involves planting the seeds directly into the soil, eliminating the need for seedlings. The technique is beneficial as it saves time and resources, resulting in faster crop production. Direct seeding is useful for crops that have a short growing period, such as corn and wheat.

Direct seeding requires a minimal amount of machinery and labor, making it suitable for small-scale planting. The technique can produce uneven plant stands, which can affect crop yields negatively.

Seed harvesting techniques are essential for ensuring the viability of seeds for future generations. The techniques vary according to the type of crop, the environment, and the desired outcomes. Manual seed harvesting, machine seed harvesting, seed stripping, seed beating, dry casting, wet casting, and direct seeding are some of the most common seed harvesting techniques.

Understanding the advantages and disadvantages of each technique is essential in choosing the most suitable technique for a particular crop, environment, and desired outcome. With the growing concern over climate change, it is crucial to use sustainable seed harvesting techniques that promote biodiversity and conservation.

Chapter 6: Proper Timing for Seed Harvest

Planting seeds can be one of the most exciting and rewarding experiences for a gardener or farmer. It is the start of new life, and with a little care and attention, these tiny seeds can grow into vibrant, productive plants. But just as important as the act of planting seeds is the timing of the seed harvest. Harvesting seeds at the right time can mean the difference between success and disappointment in your gardening or farming season. In this chapter, we will explore the proper timing for seed harvest and how it can affect the success of your plants.

Seed Harvesting Basics

Before we dive into the specifics of timing seed harvest, it's important to understand the basics of seed harvesting. Seed harvesting involves removing mature seed heads or pods from your plants and allowing them to dry out completely before storing them. Once properly dried and stored, seeds can last for years, providing a reliable supply for future planting seasons.

Collecting seeds is easy, but knowing when to collect them can be challenging. If you collect seeds too early, they may not be mature enough to germinate. On the other hand, if you wait too long, the seeds may have already started to scatter, making it difficult to collect them. Timing is critical when harvesting seeds, and it depends on the type of plant you are harvesting from.

Annuals and Biennials

Annuals and biennials are two types of plants that live for only one or two years, respectively. These types of plants tend to flower and produce seed in their second year of growth. Harvesting seeds from annuals and biennials is relatively easy since they typically have large, noticeable seed heads.

For annuals, wait until the flower begins to wilt and dry out before collecting the seeds. Depending on the type of annual plant, this may happen anytime from mid-to-late summer or in the fall. For example, if you're harvesting seeds from marigolds, you'll want to wait until the blooms dry out and the seed heads become brown. Find the mature seed heads and either pluck them off carefully by hand or cut them off with sharp scissors.

For biennials, the timing of seed harvesting can be a bit more challenging. Biennials take two years to complete their life cycle, with flowering and seed production occurring in their second year. To harvest biennial seeds, wait until the plant has completed its cycle and the seed pods have had time to mature. The timing will differ depending on the type of biennial plant, but it usually occurs in the late summer or early fall.

Perennials

Perennials are plants that live for many years and flower annually.

They tend to produce smaller seed heads or pods than annuals or biennials, making seed harvesting a bit more challenging. Perennials can be divided into two types - those that flower in the spring and those that flower in the summer. The timing for harvesting seeds from perennials will depend on the type of plant and the time of year when it flowers.

Spring-Flowering Perennials

Spring-flowering perennials typically flower in late winter or early spring, producing seed heads shortly afterward. To harvest seeds from these plants, you'll want to wait until the seed heads are fully developed and begin to turn brown. This will typically happen in the late spring or early summer, depending on the type of plant. Some examples of spring-flowering perennials include bleeding hearts, columbines, and irises.

Summer-Flowering Perennials

Summer-flowering perennials, on the other hand, typically produce their seed heads in the late summer or early fall. To harvest the seeds, you'll want to wait until the flower has begun to wilt and dry out before collecting the seed heads. Some examples of summer-flowering perennials include black-eyed Susans, asters, and daylilies.

Trees and Shrubs

Harvesting seed from trees and shrubs can be a bit more challenging than from annuals, biennials, or perennials. Trees and shrubs can take many years to produce seed, and the seed pods may not be clearly visible. Timing is critical when it comes to harvesting seeds from trees and shrubs, and patience is key.

The timing for harvesting tree and shrub seeds depends on the species and environmental factors. Typically, the seeds are ready to be harvested when the seed pod has opened, and the seeds are visible inside. The seed pods may change color, become dry and brittle, or open with a crackling sound when they are ready.

Storage and Care

Once you have harvested your seeds, you'll want to store them properly to ensure viability. Proper seed storage starts with thorough drying. Spread your seeds out on a paper towel or screen and leave them in a warm, dry place for several days. Once dry, store your seeds in a cool, dry place. An airtight container or a resealable bag is an excellent choice for seed storage.

One of the most important factors affecting seed viability is moisture. Seeds that are exposed to moisture will sprout prematurely, reducing their viability. Storing seeds in a cool, dry place is essential. A refrigerator or freezer is an ideal location for storing seeds, as it provides a consistent low-temperature environment.

Final Thoughts

Harvesting seeds is an essential part of gardening and farming. Proper timing for seed harvest ensures that you have mature seeds that are capable of germinating and growing into healthy, productive plants. Whether you're harvesting annuals, biennials, perennials, trees, or shrubs, timing is critical. Be patient, observant, and willing to experiment to find the perfect timing for each type of plant. With a bit of practice, you'll be a master seed harvester, with plenty of viable seeds to plant for many seasons to come.

Chapter 7: Identifying Mature Seeds

Seeds are an essential component of plant life and play a critical role in the reproduction of plant species. From sunflowers to wheat and from pine trees to apples, every seed holds the potential for future plant growth. Botanists, farmers, and plant enthusiasts alike spend a significant amount of time studying the development of seeds, including identifying and harvesting mature seeds for optimal seed quality and yield.

In this chapter, we will discuss the importance of identifying mature seeds, the process of seed development, and how to recognize mature seeds through their physical appearance, weight, and other characteristics.

Why Identify Mature Seeds?

The identification of mature seeds is critical for a variety of reasons, including crop production, plant research, and preservation of genetic resources. The process of seed development in plants is complex and varies depending on the species. Each plant species has specific growth requirements, including the timing of seed maturation, which are influenced by factors such as temperature, humidity, and sunlight.

To achieve the highest seed quality and yield, farmers must harvest seeds at the correct stage of maturity. Harvesting seeds too early or too late can result in reduced yield, poor seed quality, and low germination rates, which can have a significant impact on crop production.

Additionally, identifying mature seeds is essential for plant research. Researchers must collect and document mature seeds for various studies such as the preservation of biodiversity, genetic analysis, and experimental seed propagation. Mature seeds serve as a vital resource for the preservation of plant diversity and the development of new varieties.

Stages of Seed Development

Seeds undergo several stages of development that lead up to maturation. The precise timing of these stages can vary depending on the plant species, growing conditions, and environmental factors.

The first stage of seed development is fertilization. Once the plant's ovules are fertilized with pollen, the fertilized ovule develops into a seed. During this stage, the seed is still immature and must undergo further development to reach maturity.

The next stage of seed development is embryogenesis, where the embryo inside the seed develops. During this stage, the embryo grows and differentiates into a mature plant, including the development of roots, stems, and leaves. The endosperm, which provides nutrients for the embryo to grow, also develops during embryogenesis.

After embryogenesis, the seed undergoes maturation. This stage is critical and marks the point where the seed is fully developed and viable for germination. During maturation, the seed's physical appearance and weight change, and the seed becomes dormant, ready to withstand harsh conditions until it's time to germinate.

Identifying Mature Seeds: Physical Appearance

One of the most straightforward ways to identify a mature seed is through its physical appearance. As mentioned above, mature seeds change in appearance during seed development, so it's essential to know what to look for during each stage.

Before a seed reaches maturity, the seed coat appears thin, and the seed itself is small and plump. As the seed continues to mature, the seed coat thickens, and the seed becomes more rounded and resilient.

Once the seed reaches maturity, it will have a distinct physical appearance. The seed coat should be hard and dry to the touch, and the color should match the mature color of the plant. For example, mature wheat seeds will have a golden-brown color, while mature tomato seeds will be a deep red-orange color.

The shape of the seed is also significant. Mature seeds are often round or oval-shaped, and the seed coat should be smooth and free of any blemishes or cracks. If the seed is misshapen or has any defects, it should be discarded.

Identifying Mature Seeds: Weight

Another way to identify mature seeds is through their weight. As seeds mature, they become denser, and their weight increases. This increase in weight is due to the development of the endosperm and other components that the embryo needs for future growth.

To determine the weight of a seed, you'll need a scale that measures in grams or milligrams. First, weigh a sample of seeds that you know are mature and determine the average weight of each seed. Then, weigh the seeds you want to check for maturity and compare the weight to the average seed weight. If the seed weighs the same or more than the average seed weight, then it's likely mature. However, if the seed weighs less, it's still immature and needs more time to develop.

Identifying Mature Seeds: Germination Rate

The germination rate of seeds can also be used to identify whether they are mature. Germination refers to the process where a seed begins to grow and develop into a seedling.

Mature seeds have a high germination rate, meaning they will sprout and grow into a healthy plant under favorable conditions. To test a seed's germination rate, place several seeds in a damp paper towel and seal it in a plastic bag. Keep the paper towel moist and observe the seeds for growth over several days.

If most of the seeds sprout, it's likely they are mature and ready for planting. However, if few or none of the seeds sprout, they may be immature or have poor seed quality.

Identifying mature seeds is critical for successful plant reproduction, research, and crop production. By understanding the stages of seed development and looking for physical characteristics such as weight and germination rate, you can identify mature seeds with accuracy and confidence. Knowing when to harvest and store mature seeds correctly can help ensure their long-term viability and contribute to the preservation of plant diversity.

Chapter 8: Special Considerations by Plant Species

The world is a diverse place with varying attributes. In the ecological sphere, there exist different plant species, each with a unique set of characteristics, habits, location preferences, and more. In this chapter, we will dive into the special considerations that need to be taken into account when dealing with individual plant species.

Why Considerations by Plant Species Matter?

There are several reasons why such considerations are necessary. Firstly, the plants have a complex chemical and genetic makeup, making them react differently to various environmental factors such as humidity, temperature, soil type, and light intensity. Secondly, many plants have different requirements and patterns of growth, and if not given the attention they require, their potential growth or production may be limited. Lastly, plants come with various botanical properties that affect not only their growth but also their medicinal properties or commercial applications.

That said, here are the top special considerations by plant species.

1. Annual versus Perennial Plants

Annual plants, as their name suggests, have a growth habit of only one season. Therefore, for these plant species, it is essential to plant them at the right time, typically in the early spring when the soil is moist and warm enough to facilitate seed germination. Once they mature, they need to be harvested before the next winter sets in. Perennial plants, on the other hand, survive several seasons and only require pruning or cutting back in the right season, depending on their type and the environmental conditions.

2. Native versus Non-Native Plants

Native plants are those plants that are indigenous to a particular region. They have evolved over thousands of years to survive in the local environmental conditions, making them more resilient and adaptable to such conditions. Non-native plants are those that have been introduced from other regions or continents. They may require different environmental conditions, such as temperature or precipitation, to thrive, and may compete with native plants for resources, potentially disrupting the local ecosystem. Therefore, when planting non-native plants, it is essential to do so cautiously and with a clear understanding of potential benefits and risks.

3. Sun and Shade Requirements

Different plant species have different levels of sunlight requirements for optimal growth. For example, vegetables, herbs, and most fruits need full sun exposure to thrive and produce well. Trees, shrubs, and other ornamental plants, on the other hand, require varying degrees of shade (partial or full) to grow and flourish. Even at the plant level, we have variations, such as sun-tolerant versus sun-avoiding plants.

When planting specific species, it is critical to consider their sunlight requirements.

4. Soil Type and Soil Nutrients

Plants rely on the soil for nutrients and water, and different plants require different soil types and nutrient levels. For example, plants like tomatoes and peppers require a slightly acidic soil type with high levels of nitrogen, potassium, and phosphorus. In contrast, plants like blueberries and raspberries prefer a more acidic soil and require a blend of proper nutrients. Understanding the soil nutrients and pH levels required for your target plant species is critical to their growth and productivity.

5. Watering and Drainage

Water is also a vital aspect of plant growth. Different plants have different watering and drainage requirements. Some plants, such as cacti and succulents, require minimal watering and prefer dry soil conditions. Other plants need frequent watering, such as most vegetables, fruits, and flowers, to maintain a moist soil environment. Understanding and meeting the watering and drainage requirements of specific species is vital to their growth and productivity.

6. Growth Habits

Plants have different growth habits, and understanding these habits is essential for proper growth, yield, and management. We have bushy plants, ground covers, climbers, and creepers. Each type requires specific management approaches, including pruning, water, and nutrient requirements, and support. For example, climbers such as vines require support structures such as trellises or stakes to climb and produce optimally.

7. Pest and Disease Resistance

Finally, different plant species have different levels of resistance to pests and diseases. Some species have evolved to produce natural defenses against diseases or pests, while others are highly susceptible. Understanding the pest and disease resistance potential and dynamics of specific plants is essential for effective pest and disease management.

As we have seen, there are numerous considerations that one needs to take into account when dealing with different plant species. Failure to match the environmental conditions to a specific plant species could lead to poor growth, high maintenance, and yield loss. Therefore, it is vital to research and understand specific plant species' habits, growth requirements, and environmental preferences before planting and managing them effectively.

Chapter 9: Seed Cleaning Techniques

Seed cleaning is an essential process that is done before planting to ensure that the seeds are in good condition and free from any impurities or contaminants that may hinder their growth and productivity. In this chapter, we discuss several seed cleaning techniques that are commonly used by farmers and gardeners. These techniques range from simple and traditional methods to advanced mechanical processes that are used in seed cleaning factories. Regardless of the method used, the end goal is the same – to produce high-quality, viable seeds that will thrive in the right conditions.

Screening:

One of the simplest and most traditional seed cleaning techniques is screening. This method involves passing the seeds through a mesh screen that is fine enough to filter out any debris, but large enough to allow the seeds to pass through. The screens used can vary in size depending on the seed type, and they can be made of different materials such as stainless steel, brass, or nylon.

To screen the seeds, a farmer or gardener would typically pass the seeds through the screen several times, using progressively finer screens each time. This process helps to remove any large impurities such as stones, sticks, or pieces of plant material that may have been mixed with the seeds. The final screening will usually involve a mesh screen that is fine enough to separate the seeds based on size, which is important for planting and can increase the yield of the crop.

Gravity Separation:

Another traditional seed cleaning technique is gravity separation. This method makes use of the natural differences in weight between different seed components such as the seed itself, seed coats, and debris. By relying on gravity, the lighter components are separated from the heavier components, making it easier to remove impurities such as broken seeds, dust, and chaff.

To use gravity separation, the farmer or gardener would typically place the seed mixture in a container and subject it to a controlled flow of air. As the air flows through the mixture, the lighter components are lifted and carried away while the heavier seeds settle to the bottom of the container. The separated components can then be removed, leaving the seeds clean and free from impurities.

Centrifugal Separation:

Centrifugal separation is a more advanced seed cleaning technique that is commonly used in seed cleaning factories. This method uses centrifugal force to separate the seed from other components and impurities based on differences in weight, size, shape, and density. Centrifugal separation can be more efficient than gravity separation, and it can handle larger seed volumes in a shorter amount of time.

To use centrifugal separation, the seed mixture is placed in a rapidly spinning drum. The centrifugal force causes the seeds to separate from other components based on their weight and size, and they are collected in a separate chamber. The debris and impurities are also separated from the seeds based on their lightness, size, and density, and they are collected in a separate chamber or expelled from the machine altogether.

Magnetic Separation:

Magnetic separation is a technique that is used to remove metallic impurities from seed batches. This method makes use of the principles of magnetism to attract and remove ferrous and non-ferrous metal particles from the seed mixture. Magnetic separation is commonly used in seed cleaning factories, especially those that process large quantities of seeds.

To use magnetic separation, the seed mixture is passed through a magnetic separator that contains a powerful magnet. As the mixture passes through the magnetic field, the metallic particles are attracted to the magnet and separated from the seed. This method is highly effective in removing metallic impurities, but it may not be suitable for all seed types.

Air Aspiration:

Air aspiration is a seed cleaning technique that makes use of an air stream to gently remove lighter materials such as dust, chaff, and broken seeds from the seed mixture. This is done by introducing the seed mixture to an air stream that carries the impurities away while the heavier seeds settle on a vibrating conveyor or tray.

To use air aspiration, the seed mixture is typically placed on a vibrating conveyor or tray that is equipped with a fan or blower. The air stream is directed towards the seed mixture at a low velocity, and the lighter materials are carried away while the heavier seeds settle on the conveyor or tray. This method is highly effective in removing dust, chaff, and other light impurities, and it is commonly used in seed cleaning factories.

Seed cleaning is a critical step in ensuring the health and productivity of crops and gardens. The techniques discussed in this chapter have been used by farmers and gardeners for generations and have continued to evolve with the aid of technology. Regardless of the technique used, seed cleaning is a process that requires careful attention to detail, patience, and knowledge of the seed type and its unique requirements. By using these techniques, you can produce high-quality, viable seeds that will thrive in the right conditions and provide you with a bountiful harvest.

Chapter 10: Winnowing Process

Through the ages, man has developed different techniques to separate one substance from another. The separation of wheat from chaff, or garbage from recyclables, is not an easy task. For example, in ancient times, people used manual labor to separate wheat from chaff. They would throw the mixture up into the air so that the wind could carry the lighter chaff to the side, leaving the much heavier wheat grains on the ground.

As time passed, new technologies such as sieves, fans, and centrifuges emerged to replace the use of manual labor in the winnowing process. The objective remained the same: to separate a desired product from unwanted materials. In this chapter, we will explore the winnowing process, its different techniques, and the factors that impact its efficiency.

Understanding the Winnowing Process

The term 'winnowing' refers to a method of separating unwanted materials from desired grains, seeds, or other substances by using wind or air currents. The winnowing process involves blowing the mixture of materials, such as wheat and chaff, or lightweight plastic and paper, to generate a separation of the unwanted materials.

This process works by utilizing the differences in weight and size between the desired and undesired materials. The lighter substances are carried away by the wind or air currents, while the heavier ones tend to drop down to the ground. Thus, the winnowing process is a process of mechanical separation.

The winnowing process involves several factors, including the weight and size of the materials, the wind speed, and the angle of the throwing or separation device. If the materials are of different sizes, the desired product must be uniformly sized so that the separation can be carried out. Otherwise, the process may not be efficient, and the desired substance could be mistakenly carried away by the air currents.

Techniques of Winnowing

The winnowing process is commonly used in different fields, such as agriculture, food processing, and waste management. There are different winnowing techniques that are applied to specific materials and conditions. Some of the most commonly used techniques include:

Hand winnowing: This is the oldest method of winnowing, and it involves using bare hands to throw a mixture of materials, such as rice and bran or wheat and chaff, against the wind. The larger and heavier grains fall to the ground, while the lighter and smaller ones are carried away by the wind.

Gravity separation: This technique is used when the desired material is denser than the undesired one. It involves dropping the mixture through a vertical channel or inclined plate to separate the materials based on their density.

Sieve winnowing: This method involves using a sieve or mesh screen to separate the mixture of materials. The sieve's holes are made smaller than the desired substance and larger than the undesired material. The mixture is then poured into the sieve, and the screen is shaken so that the undesired materials fall through the holes, leaving the desired substance on the sieve.

Fan winnowing: This method involves using a fan or blower to blow air across the mixture of materials. The air currents carry away the lighter and smaller-sized undesired materials, leaving the heavier desired product behind.

Centrifugal winnowing: This technique utilizes the centrifugal force to separate substances with different densities. A rotating centrifuge is used to generate the force, which separates the heavier and denser materials from the lighter ones.

Factors that Affect the Winnowing Process

The efficiency of the winnowing process depends on several factors, including the properties of the materials, equipment used, and environmental conditions. Here are some of the critical factors that impact the winnowing process:

Size and weight of the materials: The size and weight of the materials determine the equipment used in the winnowing process, the throwing angle, and the intensity of the wind or air currents required for the separation. Lighter materials require higher wind or air currents, while heavier materials may not require as much energy.

Wind or air currents: The wind or air currents are crucial in the winnowing process since they carry the undesired materials away while allowing the desired substance to stay. The velocity of the wind or air currents should be carefully adjusted based on the properties of the materials and the equipment used to ensure optimal separation.

Angle of throwing or separation: The angle of throwing or separation device is critical in the winnowing process. The angle of separation equipment determines how far the materials are thrown, how long they remain in the air, and the direction of the wind or air currents. Improper throwing angles can lead to reduced separation efficiency.

Equipment used: Different equipment is used in the winnowing process, including fans, sieves, gravity separation equipment, centrifugal machines, and manual labor. The equipment used determines the efficiency of the process, the duration required, and the amount of energy needed.

Environmental conditions: Environmental conditions such as humidity, temperature, and wind speed can affect the winnowing process. High humidity can cause clumping of materials, making it challenging to separate them, while high temperatures could lead to a reduction in the efficiency of the process.

Applications of Winnowing Process

The winnowing process has a wide range of applications in different fields, including:

Agriculture: The winnowing process is commonly used in agriculture to separate grains, seeds, and wheat from the chaff, straw, or other debris. The process optimizes the farming process, ensuring that farmers save on time and get cleaner and improved quality grains.

Food processing: The food processing industry utilizes the winnowing process to separate raw materials such as nuts, cereal grains, and spices from the shells, husks, or other debris.

Waste management: The winnowing process is often applied in waste management to separate organic from inorganic materials and recyclables from non-recyclables.

Mining: The mining industry uses the winnowing process to separate metal ores from waste rock, soil, and other debris.

The winnowing process is a critical technique for separating materials of various sizes and densities. Through technological advancements, the process has been optimized, leading to increased efficiency and accuracy. Factors such as equipment used, wind or air currents, and environmental conditions play a crucial role in the success of the winnowing process.

The winnowing process has diverse applications in agriculture, food processing, waste management, and mining. It plays a critical role in optimizing operations, ensuring cleaner products, and reducing costs. As technology continues to evolve, the winnowing process is expected to become even more efficient, productive, and sustainable in the years to come.

Chapter 11: Air Drying Seeds

Seeds are the beginning of life. They are the tiny containers that carry the genetic material of plants and allow them to reproduce. Seeds come in many shapes and sizes, but they all have one thing in common: the need for proper storage. To ensure that seeds remain viable and ready for planting, proper drying is essential.

Air drying is one of the most effective and natural ways of drying seeds. It is a simple and cost-effective process that can be done without any special equipment. Air drying can preserve the viability of seeds for many years, ensuring that they can be planted when the time is right.

In this chapter, we will explore the art of air drying seeds. We will discuss the benefits of air drying, the steps involved, and how to store the seeds once they have been dried. Whether you are an experienced gardener or a novice, air drying seeds is an essential skill that you will find useful for many years to come.

Benefits of Air Drying Seeds

Air drying seeds has many benefits over other seed drying methods. The most significant benefit of air drying is its simplicity. Unlike other methods that require specialized equipment like ovens or dehumidifiers, air drying can be done without any special tools. All you need is a dry and well-ventilated area to hang or spread the seeds.

Another benefit of air drying seeds is that it preserves the seed's integrity. Many other drying methods, such as using an oven, can cause damage to the seed's genetic material. Overheating seeds can reduce their viability and make them less likely to germinate.

Air drying is also more economical. Most other drying methods require specialized equipment that can be expensive to purchase and operate. Air drying, on the other hand, only requires a dry and well-ventilated area, which is readily available in most homes.

Steps to Air Drying Seeds

The steps involved in air drying seeds are simple. Here are the most important steps to follow when air drying seeds:

Step 1: Harvesting the Seeds

The first step in air drying seeds is harvesting them. It is important to harvest seeds when they are mature, which varies depending on the plant. Mature seeds will typically be dry and have a hard outer shell. If the seeds are still moist and plump, they may not be mature enough to dry.

Harvesting seeds is also about timing. You should harvest seeds after the plant has flowered and the seed pods have begun to dry. Once the pods have fully dried out and turned brown, it is time to harvest the seeds.

Step 2: Cleaning the Seeds

Once you have harvested the seeds, you need to clean them. Remove any plant material or debris from the seeds, such as leaves, stems, or other plant matter. You can use a strainer or a sieve to help with the cleaning process.

Step 3: Drying the Seeds

Once the seeds have been cleaned, spread them out in a dry and well-ventilated area. You can use a mesh screen or a paper towel to help absorb any moisture. Make sure the seeds are spread out evenly and not piled on top of each other.

If the seeds are small, you can place them in a paper envelope or a mesh bag to hang. This will help ensure proper air circulation around the seeds. When hanging seeds, make sure there is enough space between them to prevent any mold growth.

Step 4: Checking for Dryness

After several days, check the seeds to see if they are dry. To check for dryness, try breaking a seed in half. If it breaks cleanly and doesn't bend, it's dry. If it is still flexible or bends easily, it needs more time to dry.

Step 5: Storing the Seeds

Once the seeds are dry, it's time to store them. Store the seeds in an airtight container, such as a glass jar or a plastic bag. Make sure the container is labeled with the seed's name and the date it was harvested. Store the container in a cool, dry place away from direct sunlight.

Tips for Air Drying Seeds

The following are some tips for air drying seeds:

- Humidity is the enemy of seed drying. Make sure the area you are using for drying seeds is dry and well-ventilated.
- Print out labels or tags for your seeds and attach them to the container. This will help you identify the seeds quickly and prevent any confusion.
- Take precautions against mold and mildew. Make sure the seeds are spread out evenly and not piled on top of each other. You can also apply a small amount of fungicide to the seeds to prevent mold growth.
- Be patient. Seed drying can take several days to several weeks, depending on the plant. Rushing the process can reduce the seed's viability and affect germination rates.

Air drying seeds is a simple and cost-effective way to preserve seed viability for years to come. Once you have learned the basics of air drying seeds, you will be able to store seeds efficiently and easily. By following the steps outlined in this chapter, you will ensure that you have a steady supply of viable seeds for your garden or farm.

Chapter 12: Storing Seeds for Short Term

When it comes to gardening, one of the most important things to keep in mind is that the success of your crops depends on the quality of your seeds. In order to ensure a bountiful garden, it's important to store your seeds properly. There are a variety of methods for storing seeds, but in this chapter, we will focus specifically on storing seeds for short term.

First, let's define what we mean by short term storage. This is typically a period of up to a year or two. If you plan to save seeds for longer periods of time, you will need to take additional steps to ensure their viability. But for short term storage, there are a few simple things you can do to ensure your seeds remain healthy and viable.

The first step is to make sure your seeds are completely dry before you store them. This is important because any moisture left in the seeds can lead to mold or rot, which can quickly kill off your seeds. To check if your seeds are dry, you can perform a simple test. Place a few seeds on a paper towel and let them sit for a few minutes. If the seeds leave a mark on the towel, they are still too wet to store. You can dry them out further by leaving them on a dry paper towel in a warm, well-ventilated area for a few days.

Once your seeds are dry, you can store them in a variety of containers. The most common method is to use small paper envelopes or plastic bags. Be sure to label each envelope with the type of seed and the date you collected or purchased them. This will make it easier to keep track of your seeds and ensure you use them before they expire.

If you plan to store your seeds in a plastic bag, it's a good idea to add a small amount of desiccant to the bag. A desiccant is a substance that absorbs moisture from the air, which can help keep your seeds dry. You can make your own desiccant by placing a small amount of powdered milk, silica gel, or rice in a small paper envelope and placing it in your seed storage bag. Just be sure not to place the desiccant directly in contact with your seeds, as it can absorb too much moisture and damage them.

Another option for short term seed storage is to use a sealed glass jar. This method is especially useful if you have a large amount of seeds to store or if you want to keep them organized by type. Simply place your dry seeds in a clean glass jar and seal it with a tight-fitting lid. You can also add a desiccant to the jar to help keep your seeds dry. Just be sure to label the jar with the type of seed and the date you collected or purchased them.

It's important to keep in mind that not all seeds are created equal when it comes to storage. Some seeds will remain viable for longer periods of time than others. For example, bean seeds can remain viable for up to three years, while tomato seeds are only good for about two years. Additionally, some plant varieties produce seeds that are inherently more resilient than others. When selecting seeds for storage, it's a good idea to choose high-quality seeds from reputable sources to ensure they have the best chance of remaining viable.

In addition to proper storage, there are a few other things you can do to increase the likelihood that your seeds will remain viable. One important step is to avoid exposing your seeds to extreme temperatures or moisture during the germination process. This can cause the seeds to go dormant or even die before they have a chance to sprout. To avoid this, be sure to follow the specific planting instructions for each variety of seed you are planting.

Another important factor is choosing the right time to plant your seeds. Planting too early or too late can also affect the viability of your seeds. It's important to research the specific planting requirements for each type of seed you plan to use and to plant them at the appropriate time.

Storing seeds for short term can be a simple and effective way to ensure the success of your garden. By following a few simple steps and choosing high-quality seeds from reputable sources, you can help ensure that your seeds remain viable and healthy for up to a year or two. Whether you're an experienced gardener or just starting out, taking the time to properly store your seeds can make a big difference in the success of your garden.

Chapter 13: Storing Seeds for Long Term

Save the seeds, save the planet. That may be a bit too dramatic, but seed preservation certainly plays a vital role in sustaining agriculture and ensuring food security. Seeds are not just miracle capsules that hold the potential of creating food. They are living organisms that can be genetically modified, contaminated, or lost. Preserving them for the long term is, therefore, crucial for genetic diversity and sustainable farming practices.

In this chapter, we'll look at the reasons for seed preservation and the best practices for storing seeds for the long term.

The Importance of Seed Preservation

1. Genetic Diversity

One of the primary reasons for preserving seeds is to maintain genetic diversity. Just like how biodiversity is essential for a healthy environment, genetic diversity is essential for agriculture. Preserving seeds helps maintain the original genetic makeup of crops, including for rare and endangered plant varieties. Genetic diversity also plays a significant role in crop resilience, meaning that plants are better able to withstand pests, diseases, and changing climate conditions.

2. Food Security

Preserving seeds is essential to ensure that our future food supply is safe and accessible. By preserving the genetic diversity of crops, the potential for crop losses due to disease, pests, and extreme weather is significantly reduced. This, in turn, helps ensure continued access to healthy and nutritious foods, even in times of hardship.

3. Maintaining Cultural Heritage

Preserving seeds helps to protect and maintain traditional crops that are significant to certain regions and their cultural heritage. These crops may also have unique flavors, nutritional value, and medicinal properties that would otherwise be lost. Preserving traditional crops through seed preservation ensures that they remain available for future generations.

Preparing Seeds for Long-term Storage

1. Harvesting

When harvesting seeds, it's best to choose mature, disease-free plants. It's also essential to avoid using chemical fertilizers or pesticides in the growing process. Once the seeds are ready for harvest, it's best to leave them to dry in the sun. This allows the seeds to mature and dry out naturally, making them less susceptible to mold or rot.

2. Cleaning

Before storing seeds, it's crucial to clean them to remove any remaining plant matter. This can be done by using a sieve or colander to sift out the debris. If the seeds are particularly small, using a fine mesh screen or cheesecloth will help. Be sure to remove any non-seed plant matter to reduce the risk of mold and rot during storage.

3. Labeling

To keep the seeds organized and easily identified, it's essential to label them accurately. Labeling should include the plant species, harvest date, location, and any other relevant information. You can use a permanent marker or a label maker to ensure the label won't rub off during storage.

Best Practices for Storing Seeds

1. Temperature

Seeds are living organisms that are sensitive to temperature changes. Extreme temperatures can damage the seeds' genetic structure and reduce their viability. Therefore, it's ideal to store seeds in a cool, dry, and dark place. The optimal temperature for storing seeds is between 32°F (0°C) and 41°F (5°C).

2. Humidity

Seeds are also sensitive to humidity. High humidity can cause mold, rot, and other issues. Therefore, it's best to store seeds in airtight containers with desiccants to control humidity levels. Desiccants such as silica gel or dried rice can absorb moisture and keep humidity levels low.

3. Light

Seeds are also sensitive to light. Exposing them to light for extended periods can cause a decline in their viability. Therefore, it's best to store seeds in a dark room or container.

4. Containers

Another crucial factor in seed storage is the type of container used. The ideal container for seed storage is one that is airtight, moisture-resistant, and can keep out light. Glass jars or plastic containers with lids that snap shut tightly can work well. Vacuum-sealed bags can also be used to reduce the amount of air and moisture that comes into contact with the seeds.

5. Rotation

While seeds can be stored for a long time, it's essential to rotate stored seed every five to ten years. This ensures that you are using fresh, viable seeds when planting and avoids the potential for decreased germination rates.

Seed Preservation Methods

1. Refrigeration

Refrigeration is one of the best methods for storing seeds for the long term. By keeping seeds in a cool and dark environment, they can maintain high viability rates for many years. Seed packets or glass jars with tight-fitting lids can be stored on the lower shelves of the refrigerator, where the temperature is most stable.

2. Freezing

Freezing is another method for storing seeds for the long term. However, it is essential to use a moisture-resistant container to avoid frost and ice buildup, which can damage the seeds. Label the container and keep it in the freezer's back, where the temperature is most stable. Before planting frozen seeds, it is essential to thaw them out slowly to avoid shock damage.

3. Drying

Another seed preservation method is to dry the seeds out completely. Dry seeds can be stored in airtight containers, like glass jars, plastic containers, or vacuum-sealed bags. Dried seeds can last for many years, depending on the quality and preservation method of the seeds.

4. Seed Banks

Seed banks are institutions that collect and preserve seeds for future generations. Seed banks aim to maintain genetic diversity, protect against crop loss, and support research and development into crop improvement. Seed banks store seeds in specialized facilities that can maintain controlled temperature and humidity levels, ensuring optimal seed preservation conditions.

Preserving seeds for the long term is essential for genetic diversity, food security, and maintaining cultural heritage. By following best practices for harvesting, cleaning, labeling, and storing seeds, you can ensure that your seeds stay viable and ready for planting for many years to come. Whether it's refrigeration, freezing, drying, or seed banks, there are various methods for preserving seeds. Understanding the importance of seed preservation and utilizing the best practices for seed storage can help ensure a more sustainable future for agriculture.

Chapter 14: Correct Temperature for Seed Storage

Seed storage is an essential aspect of plant conservation, biodiversity protection, and crop improvement efforts. Seed storage involves preserving the genetic diversity of plants through the collection and storage of seeds. However, storing seeds is more than just keeping them in a container. Proper storage conditions are necessary to maintain the viability, vigor, and genetic integrity of seeds. One of the critical factors that determine seed storage success is temperature. In this chapter, we will discuss the correct temperature for seed storage.

Factors that Affect Seed Storage

The longevity and quality of seeds depend on various factors that affect seed storage. Some of these factors include moisture, light, temperature, and oxygen. The optimal conditions for seed storage largely depend on the seed's species, age, and physiological state. However, among these factors, temperature is the most crucial determinant because it affects many seed processes, such as germination, respiration, and deterioration.

Temperature and Seed Storage

Temperature is a significant factor that affects seed viability, longevity, and germination capacity. When seeds are exposed to high temperatures, they lose moisture rapidly, and their metabolism accelerates. This increased metabolic activity causes the depletion of energy reserves and the deterioration of seed quality. Over time, high temperatures can cause irreversible damage to the embryo, which makes the seed unviable. On the other hand, low temperatures can slow down the seed's metabolic activity, reduce respiration and conserve energy reserves, which enhances its longevity.

The Effect of Temperature on Seed Longevity

The longevity of seeds is the period between seed maturity and the moment when the seeds are no longer viable. The longevity of seeds varies depending on the species, some can be viable for several years, while others can only last a few months. However, maintaining seeds' viability for preserving genetic diversity and supporting plant conservation practices requires that seeds be appropriately stored.

Studies have shown that seed longevity increases with decreasing temperature. For instance, seeds stored at -20°C, which is the temperature recommended for long-term gene banks, can maintain viability for up to several decades. Conversely, seeds stored at temperatures higher than 25°C have reduced viability after only a few months. Therefore, the selection of storage temperature depends on the length of storage.

The Effect of Temperature on Seed Germination

Germination is the process where a dormant seed starts to grow and develop into a new plant. The germination capacity of seeds determines their survival and growth potential. High temperature can cause seed dormancy to break, leading to rapid seed respiration and depletion of energy reserves, while low temperature can shorten the growth rate and prolong the germination process.

The ideal temperature range for most seeds to germinate is between 20°C and 30°C. Seeds that require lower or higher temperatures to germinate are classified as thermophilic or psychrophilic, respectively. For example, bean and tomato seeds require higher temperatures (25°C-30°C) to germinate, while lettuce and carrot seeds require lower temperatures (10°C-20°C) to germinate.

The Effect of Temperature on Seed Deterioration

Seed deterioration is the gradual loss of seed viability over time due to aging and environmental conditions such as temperature, moisture, light, and oxygen. The rate at which seed deterioration occurs depends on the species, physiological state, and storage conditions. Seeds stored in high temperature and high humidity conditions degrade more quickly than those stored in optimal conditions. When seed deterioration occurs, it can lead to poor or failed germination, reduced productivity, and reduced yield.

Several mechanisms contribute to seed deterioration, including oxidative stress, free radical damage, and protein degradation. High temperature accelerates these processes by triggering the release of enzymes that break down organic molecules that make up the seed. These processes lead to a decline in seed quality, reduced germination capacity, or seed dormancy breakage.

Storage Temperature Guidelines

Depending on the species and storage duration, various storage temperature guidelines have been proposed for seed storage. The most commonly used storage temperature categories include:

1. Short-term Storage

Short-term storage is usually used for storing seeds for less than 12 months. At this stage, the seeds' viability is usually not compromised, and the primary goal is to maintain the seeds' quality until germination when conditions are appropriate. Temperatures of 0°C to 5°C are optimal for short-term seed storage. At these temperatures, metabolic activity in the seed can decline, which extends seedling vigor and allows for longer-term storage.

2. Medium-term Storage

Medium-term storage involves storing seeds for an extended period, usually up to five years. This storage period aims to maintain seeds' viability and quality until they are required for propagation or conservation purposes. For medium-term seed storage, temperatures range between 0°C to -18°C, which helps control insect and microbial populations that can compromise seed viability.

3. Long-term Storage

Long-term seed storage usually involves storing seeds for over five years. This storage system aims to preserve genetic diversity and the viability of seeds for future use or conservation. Seeds can be stored for more than five decades or even centuries depending on the species and storage conditions. The recommended storage temperature for long-term seed storage is -20°C, where little or no metabolic activity occurs. This temperature helps control moisture, insects, and microbial activities, which can promote seed deterioration.

Seed storage is an essential aspect of plant conservation, biodiversity protection, and crop improvement efforts. Proper storage conditions are necessary to maintain the viability, vigor, and genetic integrity of seeds. The correct temperature is a crucial factor in seed storage because it can affect seed longevity, germination capacity, and deterioration. Therefore, the selection of storage temperature depends on the storage period, the seed's species, and its physiological state. Proper storage temperature allows for the preservation of viable seeds for optimal germination and genetic diversity maintenance.

Chapter 15: Humidity Control in Seed Storage

Seeds are delicate organisms that require proper storage to ensure they remain viable and healthy over extended periods. Generally, the quality of seeds declines with time, leading to a loss of viability and, consequently, reduced plant growth and yield. Humidity is one of the most critical factors that affect the longevity and quality of stored seeds.

Humidity refers to the amount of water vapor in the atmosphere. In seed storage, it affects the rate of water loss or absorption by the seeds, which, in turn, affects their viability and quality. Seed moisture content is essential for seed storage, as it influences the rate of respiration, which, if not controlled, could lead to a decline in seed quality.

Therefore, humidity control in seed storage is essential to ensure seed longevity and conservation. Proper humidity control involves maintaining the seed's moisture content within an optimum range, allowing it to remain viable and healthy for long periods.

Factors Affecting Seed Moisture Content

Seed moisture content is a critical factor that affects the germination and quality of seeds in storage. It is influenced by several factors, including the species of the seed, genetic makeup, maturity, and environmental conditions. When seeds are harvested, they contain a considerable amount of water, most of which is lost during the drying process. At this point, the seeds' moisture content falls to a level where they can be safely stored.

After drying, seeds are stored at different humidity levels depending on their type and expected storage duration. Seeds that are not fully dried are typically stored at lower relative humidity (RH) of 20% to 30%, while seeds that are fully dried can be stored at higher RH levels of up to 60%.

Optimum Seed Moisture Content

Seed viability and longevity are dependent on the seed's moisture content during storage. The optimum moisture content required for long-term seed storage ranges from 4% to 12%, depending on the seed type. The ideal moisture content is determined by the seed's ability to lose or absorb moisture from the surrounding environment.

For instance, seeds with a hard outer coat, such as those from the grass family, have a lower optimal moisture content of around 4% to 6%. In contrast, legume seeds can tolerate higher seed moisture contents, up to 12%. It is essential to determine the optimal moisture content for different seed types to ensure they remain viable and healthy over long durations.

Controlling Relative Humidity in Seed Storage

The relative humidity (RH) is the percentage of water vapor that the atmosphere contains. It is a crucial factor in seed storage, as it affects the rate of seed moisture loss or gain from the atmosphere. Therefore, controlling the relative humidity in seed storage is essential to ensure the seeds remain healthy and viable over extended durations.

There are several methods used to control humidity in seed storage, including:

1. Mechanical refrigeration systems

Mechanical refrigeration systems are commonly used to control the temperature and humidity in seed storage rooms. The refrigeration system lowers the temperature and humidity in the room, allowing the seeds to remain viable over prolonged durations.

2. Desiccants

Desiccants are materials that absorb moisture from the atmosphere. They are commonly used to control humidity in seed storage rooms. Common desiccants used in seed storage include silica gel, activated alumina, and molecular sieves.

3. Air conditioning

Air conditioning is another method used to control humidity in seed storage rooms. It involves controlling the temperature and humidity of the air entering the room through an air conditioning system.

4. Evaporative cooling systems

Evaporative cooling systems are commonly used in seed storage rooms to control temperature and humidity. The systems cool the air, making it less humid, which helps seeds to remain viable over extended durations.

5. Sealed storage containers

Sealed storage containers are commonly used to store seeds at low moisture contents. The containers are airtight, keeping the seeds in a low-humidity environment, which prevents moisture from entering.

Humidity control is essential in seed storage to ensure the longevity and viability of stored seeds. Controlling humidity involves maintaining the seed's moisture content within the optimal range, thereby preventing excess water loss or absorption. Proper humidity control is necessary, depending on the seed species and storage duration, as different seeds have varying moisture content requirements. Mechanical refrigeration systems, desiccants, air conditioning, evaporative cooling, and seeded storage containers are all useful methods for controlling humidity in seed storage. With proper humidity control measures in place, the germination and quality of stored seeds can be maintained over extended periods.

Chapter 16: Proper Packaging for Seed Storage

Seeds are incredibly valuable resources, containing the genetic potential for future plant growth and crop development. Proper storage of these seeds is essential to ensure the longevity and vitality of the genetic material in the seeds. Proper storage conditions and packaging are crucial for seed storage, and it is important to know the appropriate packaging options to select for optimal seed preservation. This chapter will discuss the best practices and packaging options for seed storage.

Principles of Seed Storage

Seeds are living systems, and as such, they undergo metabolic activities that can be influenced by different biological, physical, and chemical factors. These activities influence the seed's viability, vigor, and longevity. Several parameters come into play when it comes to seed storage, including temperature, humidity, light, and oxygen. Therefore, proper storage conditions must be ensured to preserve the seeds.

Temperature

Temperature is one of the essential factors that affect seed storage. High temperatures accelerate seed aging and deterioration, while low temperatures preserve the seed's viability. According to the International Seed Testing Association (ISTA), the standard recommended storage temperature for seeds is 20°C or below. The lower the temperature, the longer the seed can be stored. However, it is essential to note that freezing temperatures can adversely affect the seed's viability; therefore, long-term seed storage should avoid freezing conditions.

Humidity

The seed's moisture content is another critical factor for storage. Excessive moisture in the seed environment creates ideal conditions for seed spoilage, while low moisture content may also cause seed desiccation and subsequent loss of viability. Therefore, seed moisture content should be maintained within the safe range for storage. The safe moisture content range for seed storage ranges between 5-10%. This can be achieved by storing the seeds in air-tight containers, accompanied by moisture-absorbing packets to keep the relative humidity levels low.

Light

Light provides an important environmental factor that can affect seed germination and seed storage. Seeds, which contain plant pigments, are sensitive to light exposure, primarily green, blue, and red light. UV light can cause seed degradation and reduce longevity. When it comes to seed storage, it's best to keep them stored in a cool, dark spot or a covered container to avoid exposure to light.

Oxygen

Oxygen is a factor that can also have an impact on seed storage. High oxygen levels can cause seed rancidity and oxidation, leading to a loss of viability. Therefore, long-term seed storage usually involves reducing the oxygen levels surrounding the seeds. This can be achieved by storing the seeds in airtight containers or using vacuum sealing techniques.

What Makes Proper Seed Packaging?

Proper seed packaging is essential to seed storage and should fulfill several criteria to ensure optimal seed preservation. Packaging should protect the seed from moisture, light, and oxygen exposure, as well as mechanical damage during long-term storage. Packaging should also be easy to use and should have a long shelf-life. Finally, it should be cost-effective and environmentally friendly. A brief overview of different packaging materials used for seed storage will be discussed below.

Polyethylene bags

Polyethylene bags are affordable and widely used to package seeds. They are available in different sizes and thicknesses, and they are usually heat-sealed or stapled closed. These bags provide an airtight seal, keeping the seeds dry and safe from external contamination. One of their disadvantages is that they are not opaque and do not prevent light exposure. Therefore, they are best used in dark seed storage facilities.

Kraft paper bags

Kraft paper bags are another commonly used material for seed packaging. They are made of natural fibers and are primarily used for short-term storage. These packaging materials absorb moisture, preventing buildup and minimizing the potential for germ growth. Kraft paper bags are also breathable, which allows for gas exchange between the seeds and the environment, while still protecting the seed from direct exposure to light. However, they are not airtight like polyethylene bags and may be sensitive to tears and moisture.

Glass containers

Another frequently used material for seed packaging is glass containers. Glass containers are airtight and chemically inert, keeping the seed safe from moisture, light, and oxygen. They are also clear and allow easy viewing and monitoring of the seeds inside. Glass containers are ideal for displaying seeds and can be a good option for home use or short-term storage. However, they can be expensive and may pose a risk of breaking during shipping and handling.

Plastic containers

Plastic containers are lightweight, portable, and cost-effective. They are available in various sizes and shapes, making them suitable for different seed storage requirements. They are also airtight and prevent moisture, light, and oxygen exposure, ensuring the seeds are safe for long-term storage. Plastic containers are also durable, and their transparency allows easy viewing, labeling, and identification of the seeds inside. One of their disadvantages is that they are not as environmentally friendly as other options and may pose a risk of warming or melting in high-temperature environments.

Foiled lined bags

Foiled lined bags are an excellent option for seed packaging intended for long-term storage. These bags are available in various sizes and are designed to be airtight, opaque, and moisture-resistant. They are made by laminating layers of foil, paper, and plastic, providing excellent protection against moisture, light, and oxygen exposure. They are also cost-effective and have a long shelf life. Foiled lined bags are also lightweight, making them suitable for shipping seeds. They have the additional advantage of being environmentally friendly as they can be easily recycled.

Seed storage is paramount to preserve the integrity of the seed genetics and ensure their potential will not diminish over time. Proper seed packaging is essential to maintaining seed quality during storage. Selecting the right packaging materials for seed storage should consider several factors, including moisture, light, oxygen, and mechanical protection. The packaging should be easy to use and have a long shelf life. The packaging options can be paper, plastic, glass, and foil-lined bags, and each has its advantages and disadvantages. A combination of these materials may be required to get the desired results or needs. It is important to note that regularly monitoring seed quality during storage is equally important and adjusting storage conditions and the packaging accordingly, such as adding or changing moisture absorbing packets or adjusting temperature and humidity. Understanding the principles of seed storage combined with proper packaging options will lead to successful seed preservation.

Chapter 17: Seed Viability Testing

Seed viability testing plays an important role in plant breeding programs, seed production, seed storage, and seed quality control. It is a crucial step in the process of producing high-quality seeds, ensuring that only viable and genetically stable seeds are planted. In this book chapter, we will discuss the different types of seed viability testing, their principles, advantages, limitations, and applications.

Seeds are the main source of propagation for most plant species. They represent the genetic potential of a plant and are essential for agriculture, horticulture, forestry, and conservation. However, not all seeds are viable, meaning they have the capacity to germinate and establish a healthy plant under suitable conditions. The viability of seeds can be affected by many factors, such as genetic variability, environmental conditions, age, handling, and storage. Therefore, seed viability testing is necessary to ensure the quality and quantity of seeds before sowing.

Seed Viability Testing Methods

There are several methods to test seed viability, ranging from simple to sophisticated, traditional to modern, and destructive to non-destructive. The choice of method depends on the purpose of testing, the type of seed, the availability of resources, and the accuracy and reliability of the results. Here are some commonly used methods:

1. Germination Test

The germination test is the most widely used method to determine seed viability. It is a simple, inexpensive, and reliable method that can be performed in the laboratory or the field. The principle of the test is to count the number of seeds that germinate and develop into healthy seedlings under a set of optimal conditions. The conditions of germination vary depending on the species, but generally, they include temperature, moisture, light, and nutrients.

The germination test can be conducted in different ways, such as the paper towel method, the soil method, or the agar method. In the paper towel method, the seeds are placed between two moist paper towels and kept in a warm, dark place for a certain period, usually 7-14 days. The percentage of germination is calculated by dividing the number of germinated seeds by the total number of seeds tested.

In the soil method, the seeds are sown into trays or pots filled with sterile soil and kept in a greenhouse or growth chamber. The percentage of germination is calculated by counting the number of emerged seedlings after a certain period, usually 10-21 days.

In the agar method, the seeds are placed on a nutrient-rich agar medium and kept in a sterile chamber or incubator. The percentage of germination is calculated by counting the number of seeds that produce roots or shoots after a certain period, usually 7-14 days.

The germination test has many advantages, such as being quick, easy, and reproducible. It can also distinguish between live and dead seeds and assess the quality of seeds based on the speed and uniformity of germination. However, the germination test also has limitations, such as being affected by dormancy, disease, pests, and other environmental factors that may not reflect the actual field conditions.

2. Tetrazolium Test

The tetrazolium test is a staining technique that involves the use of tetrazolium salt, a colorless compound that can be reduced by living cells to form a red pigment. The principle of the test is to treat the seeds with a solution of tetrazolium salt and incubate them at a certain temperature for a certain time. The viable seeds will stain red, while the non-viable seeds will remain colorless or turn brown.

The tetrazolium test can be performed on whole seeds, seed sections, or embryo sections. It is a non-destructive method that can be used to test large quantities of seeds quickly and accurately. The percentage of viability is calculated by dividing the number of stained seeds by the total number of seeds tested.

The tetrazolium test has many advantages, such as being reliable, accurate, and suitable for a wide range of crops and species. It can also detect different levels of viability, such as low, moderate, and high. However, the tetrazolium test also has limitations, such as being affected by storage conditions, seed coat thickness, and embryo size, which may affect the diffusion of the salt and the staining pattern.

3. Electrical Conductivity Test

The electrical conductivity test is a method that measures the leakage of electrolytes from damaged or dead seeds. The principle of the test is to soak the seeds in distilled water for a certain period and measure the electrical conductivity of the solution. The viable seeds will leak less electrolytes than the non-viable seeds, resulting in a lower conductivity value.

The electrical conductivity test can be performed on small samples of seeds, usually 50-100 seeds. It is a non-destructive method that can be performed quickly and easily. The percentage of viability is calculated by dividing the conductivity of the sample by the conductivity of the control.

The electrical conductivity test has many advantages, such as being sensitive, rapid, and economical. It can also detect seed damage and predict seed vigor. However, the electrical conductivity test also has limitations, such as being affected by the seed coat permeability, storage conditions, and the presence of extraneous materials.

4. X-ray Test

The x-ray test is a non-destructive method that uses x-rays to visualize the internal structures of seeds. The principle of the test is to place the seeds on a radiographic film and expose them to x-rays. The viable seeds will show a clear image of the embryo and endosperm, while the non-viable seeds will show a diffused or absent image.

The x-ray test can be used to assess the quality, viability, and internal defects of seeds. It is a non-invasive method that does not affect the germination capacity of the seeds. The quality of the image depends on the x-ray equipment, the exposure time, and the seed size and density. The percentage of viability can be estimated by the proportion of viable seeds in the sample.

The x-ray test has many advantages, such as being accurate, objective, and non-destructive. It can also detect abnormal seed structures, such as internal cavities, embryo malformations, and insect infestations. However, the x-ray test also has limitations, such as being affected by the embryonic stage, seed size, density, and uniformity, which may cause variation in the image quality.

Applications of Seed Viability Testing

Seed viability testing has many applications in agriculture, horticulture, forestry, and conservation. Some of these applications are:

1. Seed Breeding and Production

Seed viability testing is essential in seed breeding and production programs to select the best genotypes, ensure genetic stability, and optimize seed yield and quality. By testing the seeds before sowing, breeders can ensure that only viable seeds are planted, saving time, resources, and space. Seed production companies can also use seed viability testing to monitor the quality of their products and meet the demand of their customers.

2. Seed Storage and Preservation

Seed viability testing is critical in seed storage and preservation programs to maintain seed quality, prevent genetic erosion, and support biodiversity conservation. By testing the seeds before storage, conservationists can ensure that only viable, healthy, and representative seeds are conserved for the long term. Seed banks and gene banks can also use seed viability testing to monitor the longevity and viability of their seed collections and prioritize their conservation efforts.

3. Seed Quality Control and Certification

Seed viability testing is a fundamental aspect of seed quality control and certification programs to assure that the seeds meet the standards of purity, germination, and identity. By testing the seeds before marketing, seed dealers can guarantee the customers that they are buying high-quality, reliable, and proven seeds. Seed certification agencies can also use seed viability testing to verify the authenticity and quality of the seeds and enforce the legal requirements.

Seed viability testing is a crucial step in the process of producing high-quality seeds and ensuring the success of agriculture, horticulture, forestry, and conservation. It allows us to distinguish between viable and non-viable seeds, assess the quality and quantity of seeds, and select the best genotypes for propagation. There are different methods of seed viability testing, each with its principles, advantages, limitations, and applications. The choice of method depends on the purpose of testing, the type of seed, the availability of resources, and the accuracy and reliability of the results. Seed viability testing should be performed regularly, consistently, and accurately to ensure the integrity and sustainability of our seed resources.

Chapter 18: Record Keeping for Seed Saving

Seed saving is an art that requires practice and patience. However, it is also a science that requires precision and careful documentation. Without proper record keeping, seed saving can become a guessing game, and the risk of losing valuable seeds increases. In this chapter, we will discuss the importance of record keeping for seed saving and provide some guidelines on how to maintain accurate records.

Why is record keeping important in seed saving?

The primary reason to keep records in seed saving is to ensure the maintenance of genetic diversity and the availability of desirable traits in future generations. Records will allow growers to identify and track the genetic characteristics of plants and their progeny, enabling them to preserve these traits and improve them through intentional selection.

Another reason to keep records is to facilitate the sharing of seeds and the exchange of information among growers and seed collectors. An accurate record of the origin, traits, and cultural practices of seeds can help in decision-making regarding seed storage, planting, and maintenance. It can also help in the identification of new traits and the exchange of information among members of seed saving networks.

Finally, record keeping is necessary for quality control and seed certification. Having accurate records can help ensure that seed meets the required standards for quality, quantity, and purity. It can also help in the identification of seed-borne diseases, pests, and contaminants that could affect the quality of harvested seeds and crops.

What information should be recorded?

The information recorded should cover the entire seed-saving process, from the selection of parent plants to the planting of saved seeds. The following are some of the essential pieces of information that should be recorded:

1. Source of Seeds: The origin of the seeds, including the name of the variety, the source of the seeds, and the year of acquisition.

2. Parent Plants: The names of the parent plants, their genetic characteristics, and their phenotypic traits. This information can be obtained through observation of plant morphology, reproductive biology, and trait assessment.

3. Cultural Practices: The cultural practices used in the production of the seeds, including planting dates, soil preparation, fertilization, irrigation, and pest management practices.

4. Harvesting and Processing: The timing of seed harvesting, the seed yield, the seed quality, and the processing methods used, including

cleaning, drying, and storage.

5. Seed Distribution: The date and manner of seed distribution, the number of seeds distributed, and the recipient's name and address.

How should records be maintained?

Records should be maintained accurately, consistently, and systematically. The following are some guidelines on how to maintain seed-saving records:

1. Use a notebook or digital software: A notebook or digital software can be used to record the information. Ideally, the notebook should be a hard-copy bound book, with numbered pages, and the software should be dedicated solely to seed saving documentation.

2. Record information immediately: Record the information as soon as possible after observing or performing particular tasks, to ensure that the details are not forgotten.

3. Be consistent in record keeping: Use the same format, language, and style of writing throughout the notebook or software. This consistency will make it easier to compare records and identify trends over time.

4. Keep it simple: Record only essential information, to avoid information overload and reduce the risk of errors.

5. Regularly update records: Regularly review and update the information to ensure that it remains accurate and relevant.

6. Store records securely: Store the records in a safe place, and make sure that they are not lost, stolen, or damaged.

Record keeping is an essential component of seed saving, and it is crucial to maintain accurate and detailed records to preserve genetic diversity and ensure seed quality. By documenting the seed-saving process, growers can track the genetic characteristics of the plants and their progeny, facilitate the exchange of information among growers, and ensure the quality of seed. Implementing record keeping practices is a valuable investment in the future of food security and agrobiodiversity preservation.

Chapter 19: Planning for Seed Saving

Saving seeds is a noble and ancient practice that has been passed down from generation to generation. More than just a mere hobby, it is widely recognized as a critical aspect of preserving biodiversity, maintaining our food security, and protecting our environment. There is no denying that seed saving can be a satisfying and rewarding experience, but it's also a task that requires a significant amount of planning. In this chapter, we'll delve into the various considerations and steps to keep in mind when planning for seed saving.

Choosing the Right Varieties

Before we get too far into planning, it's crucial to consider which vegetable, fruit, or herb varieties are worth saving. For starters, you want to choose open-pollinated varieties that have not been genetically modified in any way. The seeds from these plants are relatively stable and will produce offspring that are similar to the parent plant. In contrast, hybrid seeds are a mix of two or more genetically different plants, and the resulting offspring will not resemble the parent plant. Therefore, it's best to avoid collecting hybrid seeds.

In addition to this, you may want to consider which varieties to save based on your specific climate and growing conditions. For instance, if you live in a hot and dry area, you might look for drought-tolerant plants. Alternatively, if you have a limited growing space, you might seek out dwarf or compact varieties that take up less room.

Factors Affecting Seed Saving

There are several critical factors and considerations that you will need to keep in mind when planning for seed saving.

Pollination

Pollination is the transfer of pollen from the male to the female flower parts, resulting in the development of a fruit or vegetable. There are two different types of pollination: self-pollination and cross-pollination. Self-pollinated plants are fertilized by their pollen, and the seed that is produced will be true to the parent plant. In contrast, cross-pollinated plants rely on bees, wind, or other pollinators to transfer pollen from one plant to another. In this case, the resulting seeds will be a mix of the two parent plants. The most common cross-pollinated vegetables include squash, cucumbers, beans, and tomatoes.

Isolation Distance

If you plan to save true-to-type seeds, you will need to ensure that your plants are isolated from other varieties to prevent cross-pollination. The distance required to prevent cross-pollination varies by vegetable species. For instance, beans and tomatoes require a minimum of 10-15 feet, whereas cucumbers can cross-pollinate up to half a mile. You might also erect physical barriers or use time isolation to keep varieties separate when planting. Additionally, it's essential to coordinate with neighbors and local growers to prevent the inadvertent intermingling of plant varieties, especially when saving unique or rare varieties.

Harvesting Seeds

The timing, method, and degree of ripeness for harvesting seeds vary widely. For example, tomato seeds should be fermented for a few days after harvesting to remove the gelatinous coating, whereas bean seeds should be left on the plant until the seed pod has dried and the seeds rattle inside. In general, seeds should be left on the plant until they are fully mature and the plants have completed their life cycle. Once harvested, the seeds should be cleaned, dried, and stored under proper conditions to maintain their viability.

Storing Seeds for Longevity

Seed storage is integral to the process of seed saving. Seeds that have been adequately stored can remain viable for many years and remain viable for several generations to come. Thus, it's critical to store seeds in cool, dry, airtight containers and to keep them in a dark, stable environment. Seeds stored in variable temperatures and light conditions will not last very long. If stored in a freezer, the seeds must be thoroughly dried before being placed in a zip-lock freezer bag or airtight container and dated.

Record Keeping

Record-keeping is essential when it comes to seed saving. It is essential to know the variety name, seed source, and the date on which the seeds were saved and any notes on the growing season, harvest period, and other pertinent information. Records will help you detect any changes in seed characteristics over time and help you choose the best plants for future generations.

Planning for seed saving is an ongoing process that requires diligence and patience. The process is not only critical for maintaining genetic diversity but could also be vital for those who lack access to their favorite seeds and plants. By choosing the right varieties to save, keeping them isolated, and carefully storing them, you can embark on a journey that will offer gratifying results. Seed saving is a skill that has been passed down for generations, one that you can continue to pass down to your loved ones. Start planning today and join the ranks of those who are preserving the future by protecting the past.

Chapter 20: Creating a Seed Saving Calendar

Gardeners have been saving seeds for centuries; it's a practice that is essential to maintain biodiversity, preserve plant species, and ensure food security. Seed saving is the process of preserving the genetic diversity of plants by harvesting seeds and storing them for future planting.

Saving seeds can be a bit challenging since each plant species has its specific requirements when it comes to the perfect seed-saving environment. That's the reason why creating a seed-saving calendar is the first and most critical step towards successful seed-saving procedures.

In this chapter, we'll discuss the reasons for saving seeds, how to create a seed-saving calendar, and the best practices to keep your seeds viable for years.

Reasons for Saving Seeds

Saving seeds has several benefits, including:

Preserve Plant Diversity

The process of seed saving ensures that we maintain the genetic diversity of plant species. For example, it's estimated that only three percent of the crop varieties that existed in the U.S. in 1900 still exist today. Therefore, seed saving helps safeguard plant varieties that may otherwise become extinct over a period.

Cost-Effective

Seed-saving is an excellent way of reducing expenses associated with gardening. Instead of purchasing more seeds each planting season, you can save and replant seeds from the plants that thrive well in your garden.

Better Nutrition

Saving seeds from your fruits and vegetables allows you to control the quality of the produce you grow. Most store-bought seeds have been bred for yield or transport, which sometimes comes at the expense of flavor and nutrients.

Grow Crops Suited to Your Climate

By selectively saving seeds from vegetables and fruits that thrive in your garden, you can create crops that are well adapted to your particular gardening climate. Over time you can develop a crop that is well suited to soils, water availability, pests, and disease in your area.

Creating a Seed Saving Calendar

Creating a seed-saving calendar is essential to keep track of planting and harvesting times to save seeds. The calendar is an essential tool for tracking and monitoring your gardening activities, ensuring you do not lose the critical harvest period, which will affect the viability and genetic diversity of your plants.

The seed-saving calendar should break down the different plant varieties into specific types and their characteristics. Before creating a seed-saving calendar, here are the key factors that you should keep in mind:

1. Seed Type

Different seeds require different seed saving protocols. Some require a dry and cool environment, while others require both a dry and a warm environment. Understanding each seed type's characteristics will guide you in the appropriate seed-saving process required.

2. Germination date

The germination date is crucial in determining when to save seeds since you can't save them before they have fully matured. Although it varies from plant to plant, seed maturity occurs three to six weeks after the flowers appear.

3. Expected harvest time

Estimating the plant's growth and its subsequent maturity is a skill
that takes time to acquire. By observing your plants and taking note
of how long it takes to reach maturity, you can predict when to
expect the fruits and vegetables to reach their peak and start saving
seeds.

4. Average frost date

Knowing the average frost date in your area helps in planning when
to sow and harvest your plants. This is especially important for
tender plants that can be damaged by frost. By saving their seeds
before the frost, you can ensure the continuation of that particular
plant species.

5. Storage requirements

Different seeds have varying storage requirements. Some seeds
prefer drier conditions than others. Some seeds can only stay viable
for a year or two, and others can be stored for many years. Knowing
the appropriate storage requirements will influence when you
harvest and save your seeds and how you store them to maintain
their viability.

Best Practice for Seed Saving

1. Avoid Hybrids

Avoid saving seeds from hybrid plants since they don't typically reproduce true to their particular variety. Hybrids are created by cross-breeding different varieties to create specific traits that improve yield, size, and lifespan. Therefore, when saving seeds, use only heirloom or open-pollinated plant seeds since they will produce offspring that are true to their type.

2. Choose healthy Plants

It's essential to save seeds from healthy plants since these plants have survivor traits, which enable them to adapt to their growing conditions, resist disease and pests. Plants exposed to harsh environments and different moisture conditions are often hardier than plants grown in ideal conditions.

3. Use Clean and Dry Tools

Ensure all your tools are clean and dry before harvesting seeds to prevent contamination or rotting. Moisture is one of the leading causes of seed spoilage, so make sure to dry your harvested seeds well before storing them.

4. Label and Date Your Seeds

Labeling and dating your seeds is vital in keeping track of their viability and storage requirements. Store your seeds in containers that are airtight and labeled correctly to avoid confusing them with other varieties.

Seed saving is an essential part of gardening, and its significance cannot be overstated. By creating a seed-saving calendar, you can maintain the genetic diversity of plant species, reduce gardening expenses, and grow crops best suited to your climate.

The seed-saving calendar helps identify the different plant varieties, their growth patterns, and storage requirements, which are essential factors in determining when to harvest and save seeds. Adhering to proper seed-saving protocols, such as using healthy plants, clean and dry tools, correct labeling, and storage procedures, helps maintain seed viability for years.

Saving seeds may look like a daunting task, but it's an excellent way to preserve plant diversity, secure food sources, and save money. Make seed saving part of your gardening routine, and you will enjoy the satisfaction of growing food and flowers with your own saved seeds while preserving plant varieties that might otherwise become extinct.

Chapter 21: Cross-Pollination and Isolation

Cross-pollination and isolation are two key concepts in the world of botany. Cross-pollination refers to the transfer of pollen from a male flower to a female flower of a different plant. The process is essential in fertilization, reproduction, and genetic diversity in plants. On the other hand, isolation is the separation of plant populations from each other, either geographically, ecologically, or genetically. Isolation can occur naturally or through human intervention, and it has a significant impact on the evolution of plant species. This chapter will explore the relationship between cross-pollination and isolation and their impact on the world of botany.

Cross-Pollination

Cross-pollination is an integral part of plant reproduction. The process involves the transfer of pollen grains from an anther of a male flower to the stigma of a female flower of a different plant. The process can occur through various means, such as wind, water, or insects. Insects, such as bees, butterflies, and moths, are the primary agents of cross-pollination. They visit flowers to feed on nectar and pollen while inadvertently carrying pollen from one flower to another.

Cross-pollination plays a crucial role in plant adaptation and evolution. Through cross-pollination, plants can exchange genetic information, resulting in increased genetic diversity. Genetic diversity is essential for plant populations to adapt to changing environmental conditions, such as temperature, rainfall, and soil quality. For example, some plants can only grow in certain soil types, and cross-pollination between plants with different genetic traits can result in offspring that can thrive in different soil types.

Several advantages of cross-pollination include:

1. Increased genetic diversity: Cross-pollination results in genetically diverse offspring, increasing the chances of survival and adaptation in changing environments.

2. Disease and pest resistance: Plants with genetic diversity are less susceptible to diseases and pests than genetically uniform plants, as diseases and pests are less likely to affect plants with different genetic traits.

3. Improved yield: Cross-pollination increases genetic diversity, and this can lead to better crop yields. For example, hybrid corn varieties produced through cross-pollination are known to have higher yields than traditional varieties.

4. Pollination assurance: Cross-pollination by insects such as bees, butterflies, and moths ensures that the plants are pollinated, and reproduction occurs. This, in turn, leads to the production of fruits and seeds.

Isolation

Isolation in plants refers to the separation of plant populations from each other either geographically, ecologically, or genetically. Isolation can occur naturally, such as when a river or a mountain range separates two populations of plants, or it can occur through human intervention, such as habitat fragmentation and introduction of non-native plants.

Isolation can have a significant impact on the evolutionary trajectory of plant species. Isolation can lead to the divergence of two plant populations, resulting in the development of different genetic traits, physiological capabilities, and morphology. The divergence can result in the development of new plant species, as the two populations adapt to their respective environments.

There are three main types of isolation:

1. Geographical isolation: This occurs when two populations of plants are separated by a natural barrier, such as a mountain range, a river, or an ocean.

2. Ecological isolation: This occurs when two plant populations occupy different ecological niches, such as different types of soil, temperature regimes, or rainfall patterns.

3. Reproductive isolation: This occurs when two plant populations

cannot interbreed due to behavioral, physiological or structural barriers.

Isolation can have several advantages, including:

1. Speciation: Isolation can lead to the development of new plant species through genetic divergence and adaptation.

2. Reduced gene flow: Isolation also reduces gene flow between plant populations, which can reduce the incidence of genetic diseases and improve plant resilience to environmental disturbances such as drought or flooding.

3. Unique adaptations: Isolated plant populations can develop unique adaptations to their environments, which can lead to increased survival and reproductive success.

However, isolation can also have several disadvantages, including:

1. Genetic drift: Isolated populations of plants can experience genetic drift, where the frequencies of alleles can change randomly over time, leading to the loss of genetic diversity.

2. Inbreeding depression: Small, isolated populations of plants are prone to inbreeding depression, where the accumulation of deleterious alleles leads to reduced fitness and increased susceptibility to diseases and pests.

3. Extinction: If isolated populations of plants are too small, they may be at risk of extinction due to genetic factors or environmental disturbances.

Relationship between Cross-Pollination and Isolation

Cross-pollination and isolation are interconnected concepts in plant evolution and adaptation. Cross-pollination increases genetic diversity, and genetic diversity is essential for plant populations to adapt to changing environmental conditions. However, isolation can reduce gene flow between plant populations, which can also increase genetic diversity through genetic divergence and adaptation.

The relationship between cross-pollination and isolation is complex and depends on several factors, such as the mechanism of pollination, the type of isolation, and the geographical and environmental context. For example, if two plant populations are geographically isolated, cross-pollination may not occur, or it may occur to a limited extent if the distance between the populations is too great for insect pollination. In this case, genetic divergence and adaptation may occur due to the different environmental conditions experienced by the two populations.

On the other hand, if two plant populations are ecologically isolated, cross-pollination may occur, but the offspring may not be viable due to genetic incompatibility or other reproductive barriers. This can lead to the development of different plant species over time due to genetic divergence and adaptation.

Human intervention can also affect the relationship between cross-pollination and isolation. For example, habitat fragmentation can lead to the isolation of plant populations, reducing gene flow and increasing genetic divergence. This can lead to the development of new plant species or the extinction of existing ones. Similarly, the introduction of non-native plants can lead to the hybridization of native species, leading to genetic pollution and loss of genetic diversity.

Cross-pollination and isolation are two essential concepts in botany, and they are interconnected in plant adaptation and evolution. Cross-pollination increases genetic diversity, and genetic diversity is essential for plant populations to adapt to changing environmental conditions. On the other hand, isolation reduces gene flow between plant populations, increasing genetic divergence and adaptation. The relationship between cross-pollination and isolation is complex and depends on several factors, such as the mechanism of pollination, the type of isolation, and the environmental context. Understanding the relationship between these two concepts is critical to the conservation and management of plant biodiversity.

Chapter 22: Handling Hybrid Seeds

Hybrid seeds are cultivated by crossing different varieties or species of plants in order to produce a new variety that possesses desirable traits from both parents. These seeds are a result of careful selection, pollination, and breeding processes carried out by expert plant breeders. They are used widely in modern agriculture, where they have revolutionized crop production and improved crop yields, resistance to pests and diseases, and overall quality. However, handling hybrid seeds can be quite challenging, as they require special care and attention to ensure optimal performance. In this chapter, we discuss some essential tips for handling hybrid seeds.

Understanding Hybrid Seeds

Before discussing tips for handling hybrid seeds, it's important to understand what they are and how they work. Generally speaking, hybrid seeds are produced by cross-fertilization between two genetically different plants. The resulting offspring inherit traits from both parents and exhibit superior qualities compared to their parents. Hybrid seeds are usually the result of consistent breeding techniques employed to produce seeds that are disease and pest resistant, have increased yield, vigor, and uniformity. These desirable traits work together to produce crops with higher yields, better taste, and improved nutrition profiles.

Hybrid seeds usually come in two types, F1 and F2. F1 hybrid seeds are the first-generation hybrids produced by the cross-fertilization of two different plants. F1 hybrids are usually the most desirable because they possess superior traits that are inherited from both parents. These traits show how much effort and dedication modern plant breeders have put into producing genetically superior plants. F2 hybrid seeds, on the other hand, are the offspring of F1 hybrids and tend to be less predictable, with some undesirable traits from the parent plants.

Why is Handling Hybrid Seeds Important?

With the growing demand for food and the increasing need for sustainable agriculture practices, hybrid seeds have become crucial to modern farming. Farmers use hybrid seeds for their increased yield, resilience, and tolerance to external stress factors such as pests, diseases, and adverse weather conditions. Hybrid seeds have also been engineered to be high in nutrient content, leading to better health outcomes for consumers.

Growing hybrid seeds in the farm require specialized skills, knowledge, and attention to detail. Proper handling of these seeds includes selecting the right time for planting, ensuring optimal conditions for seed germination, storage, and handling, all of which affect the overall performance of the seeds. The tips below will help farmers and gardeners handle hybrid seeds correctly, ensuring that they maximize their potential benefits during cultivation.

Tip 1: Seed Selection

When handling hybrid seeds, the first step is selecting the best. Seed selection plays a crucial role in the success of hybrid seed cultivation. Farmers should always source their seeds from reputable and certified seed suppliers. These suppliers provide tested and verified hybrid seeds that will perform well under specific farming conditions. The quality of the seeds should be checked before purchasing and for any evidence of disease, pests, or physical damage. Hybrid seeds that are perfectly healthy and undamaged will produce strong and healthy seedlings that will lead to higher yields.

Tip 2: Planting Time

The planting time for hybrid seeds depends on the variety being grown and local climatic conditions. Farmers should refer to the seed packaging or instructions provided by the seed supplier to ensure that they plant the seeds at the appropriate time. Planting hybrid seeds outside of their recommended planting time can lead to stunted growth and lower yields. Seedlings that are planted at the right time will have optimal conditions for growth, leading to higher productivity.

Tip 3: Germination Conditions

Hybrid seeds require specific conditions for optimal germination. Usually, these conditions require a well-prepared seedbed that is free of competing weeds, disease, and pests. The soil should be fertile, well-drained, and moist for the seeds to germinate. Planting too deep or shallow can affect germination rates. Small seeds tend to be planted shallower than larger seeds. Farmers should ensure that the seeds receive sufficient water and nutrients during germination to boost growth.

Tip 4: Seed Spacing

Seed spacing is an integral component of hybrid seed planting. This involves planting seeds at appropriate intervals to ensure that the plants have enough space to grow and thrive. Overcrowding seedlings can lead to competition for light, moisture, and nutrients, stunted growth, and lower yields. Proper seed spacing ensures that each plant has enough space to grow, leading to optimal growth, higher yields, and fewer pest problems in the future.

Tip 5: Watering

Consistent watering is essential for seed germination and growth. When handling hybrid seeds, it is important to ensure that they receive sufficient water throughout their growth cycle. Watering should be done adequately to ensure that the soil is moist but not waterlogged, as this can promote fungal and bacterial growth. The amount of water the seeds receive depends on the climate and soil type. In general, shallow and frequent watering is more effective than deep watering, as it ensures uniform moisture and optimal growth.

Tip 6: Pest and Disease Management.

Hybrid seeds are more pest and disease resistant than conventional seeds. However, pests and diseases can still pose a threat to hybrid seed cultivation. Farmers and gardeners should be aware of common pests and diseases affecting the specific crop being grown and take measures to prevent and control them. Pest control can be done using natural methods such as companion planting and crop rotation, or using insecticides or fungicides if necessary. Disease control involves using cultural practices such as removing infected plants, providing adequate ventilation for plants, and using disease-resistant seed varieties. Proper pest and disease control will ensure healthy and bountiful crops.

Tip 7: Soil Management

Soil preparation, fertilization and management, are crucial factors in handling hybrid seeds. Soil provides the necessary nutrients and growing conditions for hybrid seeds. Farmers should take into account soil fertility, texture, structure, compaction, and pH levels when preparing the soil. Soil testing before planting can help farmers identify any nutrient deficiencies, pH imbalances or physical deformities in the soil that can affect seed germination and growth. Proper soil management using natural or chemical methods will increase nutrient uptake, promote plant growth, and enhance yield.

Tip 8: Harvesting

Hybrid seed harvesting involves harvesting the crop when it is mature and ready to yield. Proper harvesting involves using the right equipment, harvesting at the right time, and handling the crop with care. Damaging the crop during harvesting can reduce the number of seeds produced or reduce their quality. It is essential to keep the harvested crop clean, dry and free of pests and diseases throughout storage.

Tip 9: Seed Storage

Storing hybrid seeds requires specific conditions to ensure that they maintain optimal quality and germinability. Before storage, the harvested seeds should be cleaned, dried, and sorted to ensure that they are free of any debris, disease, or pests. Seed storage humidity levels should be below 50%RH (Relative Humidity) to avoid mold growth that could affect the seed viability. Seeds can be stored in airtight containers that are protected from light, heat, and moisture. Freezing hybrid seeds helps to extend their lifespan and protect them from pests for a longer time.

Hybrid seeds have revolutionized agriculture, making it possible to improve crop yields, introduce new varieties, and increase food security. Handling hybrid seeds requires careful attention to detail, expertise, and patience. Understanding hybrid seeds, their germination, pest control, soil preparation, seed storage, and other factors, is crucial for obtaining high-quality crops. Farmers and gardeners who follow the tips above will increase their chances of producing healthy and bountiful crops, leading to a more productive and sustainable agricultural sector.

Chapter 23: Understanding Heirloom Seeds

As many people make the switch to organic and sustainable farming practices, one topic that crops up frequently is that of heirloom seeds. These non-hybrid, open-pollinated seeds are often favored by farmers and gardeners for their hardiness, flavor, and unique characteristics. But what exactly are heirloom seeds, and what makes them so special?

Heirloom seeds have been passed down from generation to generation, often being saved and stored by families and communities for decades or even centuries. Unlike commercially produced hybrid seeds, which are developed to produce crops that are uniform in size and shape for ease of transport and marketing, heirloom seeds are selected for their natural characteristics. This means that heirloom plants may have slight variations in color, flavor, and other traits, making each crop unique and interesting.

One important aspect of heirloom seeds is their genetic diversity. This means that rather than being developed to produce a single, uniform crop like hybrid seeds, heirloom plants are more likely to be adapted to local growing conditions and to have developed natural resistance to pests and diseases. This is especially important in the face of climate change and the increasing unpredictability of weather patterns. Heirloom seeds can help to maintain biodiversity and adaptability in the face of changing environmental conditions.

Another benefit of heirloom seeds is their conservation of traditional farming methods and cultural heritage. Many heirloom varieties have been grown by specific communities or ethnic groups for centuries, and their continued use helps to preserve traditions and knowledge about farming practices that might otherwise be lost. Additionally, saving and sharing seeds among neighbors and friends is an important part of many cultures, and heirloom seeds allow for the continuation of these traditions.

Despite their many advantages, heirloom seeds are not without their challenges. Due to their lack of uniformity and the need for specific growing conditions, they can be more difficult to cultivate than hybrid varieties. Additionally, because they are less commonly produced commercially, they can be harder to come by and more expensive than hybrid seeds.

That being said, there are many resources available for those looking to incorporate heirloom seeds into their farming or gardening practices. Local seed swaps and plant sales can be a great way to discover new varieties and connect with fellow growers, while online retailers offer a wide selection of heirloom seeds at competitive prices.

If you're considering planting heirloom seeds, it's important to keep a few key things in mind. First, make sure to do your research and choose varieties that are well-suited to your local growing conditions. Some heirloom seeds are better adapted to certain climates or soil types than others, so it's important to choose plants that are likely to thrive in your area. Additionally, be prepared to spend a bit more time and effort on your heirloom crops, as they may require more specialized care than hybrid varieties.

Finally, remember that the beauty of heirloom seeds lies in their uniqueness and diversity. Don't be afraid to embrace the quirks and variations that make each crop special – after all, that's what makes heirloom seeds so valuable and interesting.

In a world where monoculture and commercial agriculture dominate, heirloom seeds offer a refreshing alternative. By preserving genetic diversity, cultural heritage, and traditional farming practices, these seeds are helping to create a more sustainable and resilient food system. So whether you're a seasoned gardener or just starting out, consider incorporating heirloom seeds into your next planting – you might just be surprised by the results.

Chapter 24: Seed Laws and Regulations

Plant breeding and seed production are critical aspects of food security. The main challenge for seed producers and breeders is to select plant varieties that can adapt to various climatic conditions, pests and diseases. Seed production involves a series of steps, including pollination, harvesting, processing, and packaging. However, these steps need to be monitored and regulated to ensure that the quality and quantity of seeds produced meet the required standards. Seed laws and regulations are designed to ensure that seeds available to farmers are of high quality, free from pests and diseases, and true to type and variety. This chapter explores the importance of seed laws and regulations, their impact on agriculture, and the various measures implemented to regulate the seed industry.

Seed Quality Standards

Seed quality standards are critical in ensuring that seed produced and sold meet the required minimum quality standards. Seed quality is determined by various parameters such as purity, viability, germination capacity, and freedom from pests and diseases. Seed purity refers to the degree to which a seed is free from impurity, including other crop seeds, weed seeds, inert matter, and other crop matter. Impurities can affect seed quality and performance, reducing the yield potential and other desirable traits.

Viability and germination capacity are other critical aspects of seed quality. High-quality seeds should exhibit high germination rates and have a high percentage of viable seeds, indicating their capacity to germinate and develop into healthy seedlings. Other factors that affect seed quality include moisture content, seed size, seed health, seed treatments, and seed storage conditions.

Seed Certification Categories

Seed certification is a system that ensures that seed produced and sold in the market meet the required standards for purity, germination capacity, and freedom from pests and diseases. Seed certification programs depend on various factors such as crops, cultivars, seed class, and varieties. The following are common seed certification categories.

Certified Seeds

Certified seeds are produced and sold under strict quality guidelines and standards to ensure that they meet the required purity, germination capacity, and freedom from pests and diseases. Seed certification agencies are tasked with inspecting and certifying seed production, ensuring that certified seed produces a high yield and the desired characteristics. Certified seeds are commonly produced using high-quality parental lines, and their progeny are rigorously tested to maintain purity and quality. Typically, certified seeds are more expensive than other seed types, but they offer higher yields, improved resistance to pests and diseases, and desirable traits.

Foundation Seed

Foundation seeds are the first generation of a new variety that is tested and purified to maintain desirable traits and performance. Foundation seed is produced by selected breeder seed, which comes from the crop's parental lines. Foundation seeds are usually produced under strict quality standards and guidelines to maintain quality and purity. These seeds are typically used to produce certified seed and maintain the variety's genetic makeup.

Breeder Seed

Breeder seed is the initial generation of a new variety that is produced by the plant breeder. Breeder seeds are commonly produced under strict conditions, such as isolation from other crops, to maintain genetic purity. Breeder seed is usually produced in small quantities and is used to produce foundation seed or for further breeding work.

Plant Variety Protection

Plant breeders invest significant amounts of time and resources in developing new plant varieties with desirable traits, such as high yield, improved disease resistance, and increased tolerance to abiotic stresses such as drought and heat. Plant variety protection (PVP) is a legal framework that allows plant breeders to protect their intellectual property rights over a new plant variety. PVP is a form of intellectual property protection that grants the plant breeder exclusive rights to produce, multiply, market, and distribute the new variety.

PVP systems are designed to promote innovation in the seed industry, encourage investment in breeding research, and promote the release of new and improved plant varieties. PVP systems also ensure that farmers have access to high-quality and genetically diverse seed, which is essential for sustainable agriculture.

Seed Marketing

Seed marketing is an essential aspect of the seed industry, and it involves the sale and distribution of high-quality seeds to farmers and other stakeholders. Seed marketing regulations ensure that seed producers sell quality seeds that meet the required standards. Common seed marketing regulations include labeling, packaging, and advertising requirements.

Seed Labeling

Seed labeling is a mandatory requirement for seed producers and distributors to provide critical information about a seed product. Seed labels should provide information such as crop species, variety, and cultivar, purity, germination percentage, and the presence of any impurities or pathogens. Labeling requirements ensure that farmers make informed decisions about the seed they buy and plant.

Seed Packaging

Seed packaging plays a crucial role in maintaining seed quality, and it should protect the seed from moisture, light, and other environmental factors that can affect seed quality and viability. Packaging should also provide information about the seed product and meet specific regulatory requirements. For example, seed packaging should not contain any false, misleading, or deceptive content or graphics.

Seed Advertising

Seed advertising is a marketing tool used by seed producers to promote their products and services. Seed advertisements should not contain information that is false, misleading, or deceptive. Seed advertisements should provide factual information about the quality and performance of the seed product.

Seed Import and Export Regulations

Seed import and export regulations are designed to ensure that imported and exported seed meet specific quality and regulatory requirements. Seed import regulations usually require that the seed product undergoes various forms of testing, including genetic identity testing, purity testing, and freedom from pests and diseases. Seed export regulations are crucial in ensuring that seed produced and exported meet the quality and regulatory requirements of the importing country.

Seed laws and regulations are essential in ensuring that the seed industry operates within the required standards and guidelines. Seed quality standards, certification categories, plant variety protection, seed marketing, and import/export regulations ensure that farmers have access to high-quality, safe, and sustainable seed. The seed industry contributes significantly to food security and agricultural development, and seed laws and regulations are critical in promoting innovation, investment, and access to high-quality seed.

Chapter 25: Seed Exchange Programs

One of the most fascinating things about our planet is the abundance of plant life that inhabits it. From towering trees to shrubs, herbs, flowers and grasses, there are thousands of different species of plants all around us, each with their own unique properties and benefits.

Seeds form the foundation upon which all of these plants are built. Encased within a tough outer shell, each seed contains all of the genetic information necessary to grow into a mature plant, as long as it is given the right conditions. For many people, the process of growing plants from seed is a hobby that is both enjoyable and rewarding. However, it can also be a challenge, particularly for those who are just starting out.

Seed exchange programs offer a solution for people who are looking to grow their own plants, but who may not have access to the seeds they need. These programs enable gardeners and enthusiasts to trade seeds with each other, allowing them to expand their collection and try out new varieties that they may not have encountered before.

In this chapter, we will take a closer look at seed exchange programs, exploring their history, the benefits they offer, and how you can get started with a program of your own.

A Brief History of Seed Exchange Programs

Seed exchange programs have a long and interesting history, dating back to the earliest days of human civilization. For centuries, farmers and gardeners have been trading seeds with each other in order to grow crops that are well-suited to their local environment.

In the modern era, seed exchange programs really took off in the 20th century, as hobbyist gardeners began sharing their seeds with each other through local clubs and organizations. As the internet became more widespread, these programs were able to reach a wider audience, with many websites and online forums dedicated to seed swapping.

Today, seed exchange programs continue to grow in popularity, with thousands of gardeners participating in programs around the world. While the specifics of these programs can vary, the basic idea is always the same: gardeners trade seeds with each other, helping to expand their knowledge and create a more diverse and varied garden.

Benefits of Seed Exchange Programs

There are many benefits to participating in a seed exchange program, both for individual gardeners as well as for the wider environment. Here are just a few of the most important benefits:

1. Expand Your Collection: One of the primary benefits of seed exchange programs is that they allow you to expand your collection of seeds, giving you access to a wider range of plant varieties than you may be able to find locally. This is particularly important for rare or unusual varieties, which may be difficult to find through other means.

2. Cost-Effective: Buying seeds can be expensive, particularly if you are looking for rare or unusual varieties. By participating in a seed exchange program, you can often find great seeds for little or no cost, as you are simply trading with other gardeners.

3. Promote Biodiversity: By growing a wider range of plant species in your garden, you can help to promote biodiversity and protect the environment. This is particularly important given the increasing number of threats facing the world's plants, from climate change to habitat destruction and more.

4. Connect with Like-Minded Gardeners: Participating in a seed exchange program can be a great way to connect with other gardeners who share your interests and passions. Whether you are just starting out or are a seasoned veteran, there is always more to learn from others, and a seed exchange program provides the ideal platform for sharing knowledge and advice.

Getting Started with a Seed Exchange Program

If you are interested in participating in a seed exchange program, there are a few things you will need to do in order to get started. Here are the basic steps:

1. Find a Program: The first step is to find a seed exchange program that suits your needs. There are many different programs out there, each with their own focus and rules, so it can be helpful to do some research and find one that is a good match for your interests.

2. Prepare Your Seeds: Once you have found a program, you will need to prepare your seeds for trading. This typically involves collecting and cleaning the seeds, and then storing them in a cool, dry place until you are ready to exchange them with other gardeners.

3. Join the Program: With your seeds ready to go, you can now join the seed exchange program of your choice. This typically involves signing up online, providing some basic information about yourself and your garden, and agreeing to the program's rules and guidelines.

4. Trade Seeds: Once you are registered with the program, you can start trading seeds with other gardeners. This is typically done through an online platform or forum, where you can connect with other members and arrange to swap seeds by mail.

Tips for Successful Seed Trading

Participating in a seed exchange program can be a lot of fun, but it also requires some care and attention to ensure that you get the most out of the experience. Here are a few tips for successful seed trading:

1. Be Prepared: Make sure that your seeds are properly cleaned and organized before you trade them. This will help to ensure that they are in good condition when they arrive at their destination, and will make it easier for other gardeners to grow them successfully.

2. Be Courteous: Remember that you are dealing with other people, so it is important to be polite and courteous when you communicate with them. This means responding promptly to messages, sending your seeds on time, and being respectful of others' time and effort.

3. Be Honest: When you trade seeds with other gardeners, it is important to be honest about what you are offering. Make sure that you accurately describe the seeds you are trading, including their species, variety, and any important growing information.

4. Learn from Others: Participating in a seed exchange program is a great opportunity to learn from other gardeners. Take the time to read their advice, ask questions, and try out new varieties that you may not have encountered before.

Seed exchange programs are a wonderful way to expand your collection of plant seeds and connect with other like-minded gardeners. Whether you are a novice or an experienced gardener, there is always something new to learn through these programs, and they offer a great opportunity to promote biodiversity and protect the environment. If you are interested in growing your own plants and want to get involved with a community of other gardeners, a seed exchange program may be just what you're looking for.

Chapter 26: Building a Seed Saving Community

The practice of seed saving has been around for thousands of years and it has always been a vital part of human survival. However, the rise of industrial agriculture in the 20th century has led to a decline in the diversity of seeds and the knowledge of how to save and share them. This has created a dangerous situation where our food security is threatened by a lack of genetic diversity and the dependence on a small number of commercial seed companies. The good news is that there is a growing movement of seed savers who are working to preserve our food heritage and build resilient communities. In this chapter, we will explore the steps involved in building a seed saving community.

Step 1: Educate and Empower

The first step in building a seed saving community is to educate and empower people about the importance of seed saving and the techniques involved. This can be done through workshops, classes, and community events. The focus should be on making seed saving accessible and inclusive, regardless of prior experience, income, or cultural background. One valuable approach is to partner with local organizations and institutions, such as schools, libraries, and cultural centers, to reach a diverse audience.

Seed libraries are also an effective tool for educating and empowering people about seed saving. A seed library is a community-led initiative that allows people to borrow, grow, and return seeds. It is a simple and low-cost way to share seeds and knowledge among a group of people. Seed libraries can be started at local libraries, community centers, or even in people's homes. They can also be mobile, using a bike or a van to bring seeds and education to different neighborhoods.

Another way to empower people is to provide them with the tools and resources they need to save and share seeds. This includes seed packets, labels, envelopes, and storage containers. Seed saving kits can be distributed at workshops or available for purchase. The goal is to make seed saving an easy and accessible activity that anyone can do.

Step 2: Connect and Collaborate

The second step in building a seed saving community is to connect and collaborate with other seed savers, organizations, and institutions. This means building partnerships and networks that can support the exchange of seeds, knowledge, and resources.

One way to connect with other seed savers is through seed swaps. Seed swaps are events where people can bring and exchange seeds with others. They are a great way to meet other seed savers, learn about different varieties of seeds, and build a local seed network. Seed swaps can be organized by individuals or organizations and can take place at community events, farmers' markets, or other public spaces.

Another way to connect with other seed savers is through online communities and social media. There are many online forums and groups dedicated to seed saving, where people can ask questions, share information, and connect with others. Social media platforms like Facebook and Instagram can also be used to share pictures, videos, and stories about seed saving.

Collaboration with organizations and institutions is also important in building a seed saving community. This can include working with local farmers, seed companies, and non-profit organizations. For example, seed companies can donate excess or discontinued seeds to seed libraries or seed swaps. Non-profit organizations can provide funding or resources to support seed saving initiatives. Farmers can grow and save seeds from their own crops and share them with the community.

Step 3: Preserve and Protect

The final step in building a seed saving community is to preserve and protect the seeds that have been saved. This involves proper storage, labeling, and documentation of the seeds to ensure their long-term viability and identity.

Seeds should be stored in a cool, dry, and dark place, such as a refrigerator or a freezer. Proper labeling is also important to avoid confusion and ensure that the correct seeds are being planted. Labels should include the name of the variety, the date of harvest, and any other relevant information. Documentation of the seeds can be done through record keeping and seed cataloging software, which allows for easy tracking and sharing of seed information within the community.

Seed banks are another option for preserving and protecting seeds. Seed banks are facilities that store seeds in a controlled environment, such as a cold room or a seed vault. They are used to conserve rare and endangered varieties of seeds and ensure their availability for future generations. Seed banks can be public or private, with some being operated by governments and others by non-profit organizations.

Building a seed saving community is a vital and rewarding endeavor for anyone interested in food security, biodiversity, and community resilience. By educating and empowering people, connecting and collaborating with others, and preserving and protecting the seeds that have been saved, we can create a vibrant and sustainable seed saving culture that benefits us all. We hope that this chapter has provided you with the inspiration and knowledge to start your own seed saving community and join the growing movement of seed savers around the world.

Chapter 27: Germinating Seeds Overview

Seeds are the starting point of a plant's life, and germination is the process by which the seed begins to grow and develop into a plant. This process is essential for the success of any garden or agricultural endeavor, and understanding how it works is key to achieving healthy, robust plants. In this chapter, we will provide an overview of the germination process and explain the science behind it.

The Purpose of Germination

Germination is the first step in a plant's life cycle. The purpose of the process is to transform the dormant seed into a living, growing plant. Seeds are designed to wait in a state of dormancy until the right conditions exist for them to grow. These conditions include adequate moisture, oxygen, and warmth. When these conditions are met, the seed will begin to germinate.

The Germination Process

The germination process is a complex sequence of events that takes place in several stages. These stages include imbibition, activation, and growth.

Imbibition is the process by which the seed absorbs water. As the seed absorbs water, it begins to swell, and the outer shell of the seed expands. This is an essential step in the germination process, as it softens the outer shell and allows the seed to break through.

Activation is the process by which the seed begins to initiate growth. During this stage, enzymes within the seed start to break down stored food and turn it into energy. This energy is then used by the plant for growth.

Growth is the final stage of germination, where the root and shoot emerge from the seed. The first part of the plant to emerge is the root, which anchors the plant in the soil and absorbs water and nutrients. Once the root is established, the shoot emerges above the soil, and leaves begin to form.

Factors Affecting Germination

Several factors can affect the germination process, including light, temperature, water, and soil conditions.

Light

Some seeds require light to germinate, while others do not. Seeds that require light are often surface sown, as they need to be in direct contact with the light to initiate germination. Examples of seeds that require light to germinate include lettuce, petunias, and parsley.

Temperature

Temperature plays a crucial role in the germination process. Most seeds require a specific range of temperatures to germinate successfully. Cold-tolerant seeds, such as peas, require temperatures of around 50°F (10°C) to germinate. Warm-tolerant seeds, such as tomatoes, require temperatures of around 70°F (21°C) to germinate. Extreme temperatures can also inhibit germination. For example, temperatures below freezing or above 95°F (35°C) can damage or kill seeds.

Water

Water is essential for the germination process. Seeds require adequate moisture to soften the seed coat and initiate the germination process. However, seeds can also be damaged by excess water. If seeds are overwatered, they can rot or develop fungal diseases.

Soil Conditions

Soil conditions can also affect the germination process. Soil that is too compacted or lacks nutrients can hinder the growth of roots and shoots. Additionally, soil that is too acidic or alkaline can also affect germination. Testing soil pH and ensuring proper soil drainage are essential for successful germination.

Seed Germination Methods

Several methods can be used to germinate seeds. The most common methods are direct sowing, indoor sowing, and stratification.

Direct sowing involves sowing seeds directly into the ground or container where they will grow. This method is commonly used for seeds that are hardy, easy to germinate, or prefer not to be transplanted. Direct sowing is often used in the spring when conditions are ideal for germination.

Indoor sowing involves starting seeds indoors before transplanting them outdoors. This method is commonly used for seeds that require a longer growing season, or for gardeners who want to get a head start on their planting. Indoor sowing is often done in pots or trays with moist soil and placed in a warm, sunny location.

Stratification is a seed germination method that involves exposing seeds to cold temperatures to simulate the winter season. This method is commonly used for seeds that require a period of cold before they can germinate. Seeds can be stratified in the refrigerator or in a cool, dark location.

Common Seed Germination Problems

Several issues can arise during the germination process, including poor germination, damping off, and seedling diseases.

Poor Germination

Poor germination can be caused by several factors, including incorrect temperature, lack of water, poor soil, or low seed viability. Ensuring proper soil temperature, adequate moisture, and healthy soil can help prevent poor germination.

Damping Off

Damping off is a common seedling disease that affects the stems of newly germinated seedlings. It is caused by a fungal infection that thrives in moist, warm soil. Symptoms of damping off include thin, yellowed stems, and collapsed seedlings. Damping off can be prevented by ensuring proper soil drainage and using sterile soil or starting mix.

Seedling Diseases

Seedling diseases can affect newly germinated seeds and seedlings. These diseases are often caused by fungal or bacterial infections. Symptoms of seedling diseases include stunted growth, yellowing leaves, and rotting roots. Seedling diseases can be treated by removing affected plants and treating the soil with fungicides. Germination is a crucial process in the life cycle of a plant. Understanding the science behind germination and the factors that affect it can help gardeners achieve healthy, robust plants. By ensuring proper soil temperature, adequate moisture, and healthy soil, gardeners can prevent common germination problems and enjoy a bountiful harvest.

Chapter 28: Soil Requirements for Germination

Germination is the process by which a seed sprouts and begins to grow into a new plant. It is a crucial stage in the life cycle of plants and is heavily influenced by the conditions of the soil in which the seed is planted. In this chapter, we will discuss the soil requirements for germination and explore how different soil characteristics can affect the process.

Soil Types

There are three main types of soil: sandy, clay, and loamy. Sandy soil has large particles and is very porous, which means it drains water quickly. Clay soil, on the other hand, has small particles and holds onto water for longer periods of time. Loamy soil is a mixture of both sandy and clay soil and is often considered the ideal soil type for growing plants.

Soils with a higher clay content may not be well-suited for germination, as they can become compacted and make it difficult for seedlings to push through the soil. Soil that is too sandy may not hold enough moisture to support the germination process, causing the seed to dry out and die. Loamy soil, therefore, offers the best balance of water drainage and retention, allowing for successful germination.

Soil pH

The pH of soil refers to its acidity or alkalinity and can have a significant impact on the ability of seeds to germinate. Most plants prefer a slightly acidic soil, with a pH between 6.0 and 7.5. However, some plants may require more acidic soil, while others may need a more alkaline environment.

To test the pH of soil, a soil pH kit can be purchased at a gardening store or online. If the pH is too high or too low, it can be adjusted by adding soil amendments. For instance, to increase the acidity of soil, sulfur can be added, whereas adding lime can increase the alkalinity of soil.

Soil Nutrients

Seeds require a variety of nutrients to encourage germination and growth. Some of these nutrients include nitrogen, phosphorus, and potassium. Nitrogen is particularly important during the early stages of germination, as it encourages the development of chlorophyll, which is necessary for photosynthesis.

Phosphorus is vital for root development, which helps the plant to absorb nutrients from the soil. Potassium is often referred to as the "quality nutrient" as it improves the overall quality of the plant, including its fruit size and disease resistance.

To provide these essential nutrients to the soil, gardeners can use fertilizers or organic matter like compost. However, it is important to use these materials sparingly, as too much nitrogen, for example, can actually harm the germination process.

Soil Moisture

Soil moisture is essential for germination, as it supports the uptake of oxygen and nutrients by the seed. A lack of moisture in soil can cause the seed to dry out and die, while waterlogged soil can lead to root rot and other fungal diseases.

It is important to maintain the correct level of soil moisture during the germination process. This can be achieved by keeping the soil moist, but not soaking wet. When watering the seed, it is important to avoid getting the leaves wet, as this can encourage the growth of fungal diseases.

The type of soil and the size of the seed can also affect the required moisture level. For instance, larger seeds may require a deeper, more water-retentive soil, while smaller seeds may require a shallower soil depth with more frequent watering.

Soil Temperature

Soil temperature is an important factor in the germination process, as it affects the metabolic rate of the seed. Different plant species require different soil temperatures for germination, with some preferring cooler temperatures and others requiring warmer conditions.

Most seeds prefer a soil temperature of between 70 and 90 degrees Fahrenheit. If the soil temperature is too low, the seed may not be able to break through the soil surface, while soil that is too hot can cause the seed to dry out and die.

To maintain the correct soil temperature, gardeners can use mulch or other forms of insulation to keep the soil warm. They can also place their seedlings in areas with plenty of sunlight and good airflow, which can help regulate soil temperatures.

Soil Structure

Soil structure refers to the physical arrangement of soil particles, such as its texture and density. A soil's structure can affect the ease with which a seed can germinate and grow, as well as the availability of nutrients and water.

Soils with a loose, porous structure promote good root development, allowing the roots to grow deep into the soil and absorb nutrients. Excessive compaction of soil, on the other hand, can make it difficult for roots to penetrate the soil and absorb the necessary nutrients.

To improve soil structure, gardeners can add organic matter like compost or other soil amendments. Additionally, regularly tilling soil can help to break up compacted soil and improve drainage.

Soil requirements for germination are crucial determinants of a seed's ability to sprout and grow into a healthy plant. Soil type, pH, nutrients, moisture, temperature, and structure all play an important role in promoting the germination process.

It is important for gardeners to understand the unique requirements of each plant they wish to grow and to adjust their soil accordingly. By providing the right soil conditions, gardeners can help to ensure successful germination and healthy plant growth.

Chapter 29: Temperature Requirements for Germination

Germination is the process of a seed, spore, or bud beginning to grow and develop into a mature plant. The process of germination can be influenced by various factors, such as the availability of water, oxygen, and nutrients, as well as the temperature. Temperature is a critical factor that affects germination, as it determines the rate at which the seed absorbs water and the enzymes that break down the stored nutrients in the seed. The optimal temperature for germination varies according to the species of plant, and deviations from this optimal range can have adverse effects on the process. In this chapter, we will discuss the temperature requirements for germination and the effects of temperature on the germination of various plant species.

Temperature Range for Germination

The optimal temperature range for germination is the temperature at which the maximum number of seeds germinate, and the rate of germination is the highest. For most plant species, the optimal temperature range for germination is between 20°C and 30°C. This is because the enzymes that break down the stored nutrients in the seed are most active at this temperature range, allowing for rapid growth and development of the plant. However, some plant species can germinate at temperatures as low as 2°C, while others require temperatures of up to 40°C. There are also plants that require alternating temperatures for germination, with a period of warm and cool temperatures to break their dormancy.

Effects of Low Temperature on Germination

Low temperature affects the germination process in different ways depending on the plant species. For some plants, low temperature can stimulate seed dormancy, leading to a delayed germination process. This dormancy is a mechanism used by the plant to ensure that seeds do not germinate during unfavorable environmental conditions. In other plants, low temperature can cause physiological changes to the seed, leading to reduced water absorption, slow enzyme activity, and poor nutrient mobilization, resulting in poor germination rates. The optimal temperature can vary according to the species of plant, but for most plants, a low temperature of less than 10°C can have adverse effects on the germination process.

Effects of High Temperature on Germination

High temperature also affects the germination process in various ways depending on the plant species. For some plants, high temperature can lead to the inhibition of germination, as the enzymes that break down the stored nutrients in the seed may become denatured at temperatures above 35°C, leading to reduced water absorption and slow nutrient mobilization. In other plants, high temperature can also cause plant stress, leading to reduced germination and seedling vigor. The optimal temperature can vary according to the species of plant, but for most plants, a high temperature of more than 40°C can have adverse effects on the germination process.

Temperature Requirements for Different Plant Species

Different plant species have different requirements for temperature during germination. Some plant species require cool temperatures for germination, while others require warm temperatures. Below are some examples of plant species and their temperature requirements for germination.

Cucumber

The optimal temperature for cucumber germination is between 25°C and 30°C. Cucumber seeds will not germinate at temperatures below 10°C or above 35°C. The germination process for cucumber begins at about 12°C but at a slower rate. Cucumber seeds require moist soil and adequate sunlight for successful germination.

Tomato

Tomato seeds require warm temperatures for germination, with the optimal range being between 20°C and 25°C. Germination will not occur below 10°C or above 35°C. The seeds germinate in about five to ten days at the optimal temperature, and once the plant has developed its first true leaves, it can handle cooler temperatures of around 15°C.

Sweet Corn

The optimal temperature for germinating sweet corn is 20°C, but the seeds can still germinate at temperatures between 10°C and 32°C. Sweet corn requires adequate moisture during the germination period, and the soil temperature should be monitored to ensure that it remains within the optimal range.

Lettuce

Lettuce germinates best at cooler temperatures of between 5°C and 22°C. The seeds will not germinate at a temperature above 27°C, leading to decreased germination rates. Lettuce seeds require moist soil and adequate sunlight for successful germination.

Carrots

The optimal temperature range for carrot germination is between 7°C and 30°C. However, the best germination rates occur within the 18°C to 22°C range. Carrot seeds require moist soil and at least 16 hours of daylight for successful germination.

Effects of Germination on Temperature on Agriculture

Temperature is an essential factor that affects the germination process, and deviations from the optimal temperature range can have adverse effects on the germination rates and the overall yield of crops. High-temperature stress during germination can also affect subsequent plant growth and development, leading to reduced crop yields. In agriculture, controlling the temperature during germination is essential to ensure optimal conditions for seed growth and development, leading to increased yields and improved economic outcomes for farmers.

Temperature is a critical factor that affects the germination process, and the optimal temperature range varies according to the species of plant. Deviations from the optimal temperature range can lead to reduced germination rates, delayed germination, and reduced plant vigor. It is essential for farmers to control the temperature during germination to ensure optimal conditions and increased crop yields. The future of agriculture will depend on how well we manage temperature during germination, and innovative solutions must be developed to ensure the continued success of the industry.

Chapter 30: Water Requirements for Germination

Germination is the first step in the growth of any plant. The seed is essentially a dormant plant, and the process of germination activates the embryo, which then starts to grow into a full-fledged plant. For germination to occur, the right conditions must be present. One of the most crucial conditions is water. Water is required for the activation of enzymes that break down stored food in the seed and also for the uptake of nutrients. The water requirements for germination vary among different plant species, but there are some general principles that govern this process.

Water Availability

The availability of water is one of the most critical factors that determine the success of seed germination. If seeds do not have access to sufficient water, they will simply remain dormant. Soil moisture levels, rainfall patterns, and irrigation practices will all affect water availability. The amount of water that is needed for seed germination varies among different seeds, but it is generally agreed that seeds should be kept moist but not too wet during the germination process.

Some seeds, like beans, do not require constant moisture during germination. Instead, they only require a few hours of moisture each day. Other seeds, like lettuce, require constant moisture throughout the germination process. Seeds from arid environments, like cacti, require less water for germination than seeds from moist environments, like ferns.

Seed Coat Hydration

The seed coat is the tough outer layer that surrounds the embryo, protecting it from damage and dehydration. The seed coat also contains small pores that allow water to pass through. The hydration of the seed coat is an essential step in seed germination, as it triggers the release of enzymes that break down stored food in the seed. Different types of seed coats require different amounts of water for proper hydration.

Imbibition is the process by which water is absorbed by the seed coat and initiates the germination process. During imbibition, the seed coat swells and begins to soften. This allows the embryo to emerge from the seed, eventually growing into a new plant. Some seeds have very hard seed coats that require special treatments to break down before they can absorb water. For example, scarification is a process of mechanically breaking the seed coat in some types of seeds to allow them to absorb water.

Temperature and Water

The temperature at which a seed is exposed to water is another important factor that can influence the success of germination. Seeds require a specific range of temperatures to germinate, and water temperature plays a role in this process. In general, the temperature of the water should be just below the optimal germination temperature for the particular species of seed. This can enhance the speed and reliability of germination.

The temperature of the soil also plays a role in seed germination, as it affects the availability of water to the seed. If the soil is too cold, the water in the soil may be unavailable to the seed, even if there is sufficient moisture available. Conversely, if the soil temperature is too high, the water in the soil can evaporate too quickly, leaving the seed without adequate water.

Seed Dormancy

Not all seeds germinate immediately after exposure to water. Some seeds have built-in delay mechanisms that prevent them from germinating until environmental conditions are favorable. This is known as seed dormancy, and it is a common trait among many plant species.

During dormancy, seeds are able to remain viable for long periods, waiting for the right conditions to germinate. Dormancy can be broken by a variety of stimuli, including temperature, moisture, oxygen, light, and mechanical damage. These stimuli send signals to the seed that the conditions are now favorable for growth, and the seed starts to break down stored food to start the germination process.

The water requirements for germination are critical to the success of any plant species. Seeds require specific amounts of water to hydrate the seed coat, activate enzymes to break down stored food, and uptake nutrients. Temperature, soil moisture, and seed dormancy are also factors that can influence the success of germination. By understanding the water requirements for germination, gardeners and farmers can establish optimal growing conditions for their crops and increase their yields. In addition, understanding these requirements can help to predict which species of plants will thrive in different environments, leading to more sustainable agriculture.

Chapter 31: Light Requirements for Germination

Seed germination is the process by which a plant embryo inside a seed awakens and begins to grow into a new plant. This process is governed by a complex interplay of environmental factors and internal genetic mechanisms. One of the most crucial environmental factors influencing germination is light. Light is required for many plants to start the process of germination and it is essential for the growth and development of the newly emerged seedlings. This chapter will discuss the light requirements for germination and how different types of light affect the process.

Types of light

It is essential to understand the different types of light before delving into the light requirements for germination. Light is usually categorized based on its spectral properties, which dictates how it affects plant growth. The electromagnetic spectrum ranges from shortwave radiation, such as gamma rays and X-rays, to long waves like radio waves. However, the light range of interest for plant growth is between 400 and 700 nanometers, which is visible light.

Visible light is composed of different wavelengths, which create the different colors we can see. These colors range from violet, blue, green, yellow, orange, to red. All these colors have different effects on plant growth, but blue and red light are the most important colors for plants.

Blue light

Blue light falls between 440 and 470 nm wavelength and has different effects on plant growth and development. It is essential for chlorophyll synthesis and phototropism, which is the movement of plants towards or away from light. Blue light also plays a crucial role in regulating stomatal opening and closure, which affects gas exchange and water balance in the plant.

Red light

Red light falls between 630 and 700 nm wavelength and has different effects on plant growth and development. It is essential for the regulation of circadian rhythms and photoperiodism, which are biological processes that respond to the duration of light and dark periods. Red light also plays a crucial role in promoting flowering, stem elongation, and carbohydrate synthesis.

Light Requirements for Germination

Light plays a crucial role in the germination of many plant species. However, not all plants require light for germination, and some even require darkness. Therefore, light requirements for germination vary among plant species and are closely linked to their ecological niche. Some plants require light to break seed dormancy, while others require light to trigger the synthesis of enzymes that break down seed coats. Also, different types of light can affect germination differently.

Light type and intensity

Several factors determine the type and intensity of light required for germination. The most important ones include the sensitivity of the seeds to light, the light spectrum, the intensity of light, the duration of light, and the temperature. Blue light is essential for the germination of most vegetable seeds, while red light is most critical for the germination of seeds from flowers, trees, and most grain crops. The intensity of light required for germination varies depending on the species, and some seeds can tolerate up to 20 hours per day, while others require complete darkness.

Influence of duration of light

The duration of light also influences germination. Short-day plants require less than twelve hours of exposure to light per day to germinate, while long-day plants require over twelve hours of exposure to light per day to germinate. Intermediate-day plants require between twelve and sixteen hours of exposure to light per day to germinate. The duration of exposure to light influences the synthesis of photoreceptors, which are essential for light perception, and plant growth regulators such as auxins.

Effect of temperature

The temperature also affects the light requirements for germination, and optimal germination temperature varies depending on the species. Most cool-season crops such as peas, lettuce, and spinach require temperatures between 15-20°C for optimal germination, while warm-season crops such as cucumber, tomato, and pepper require temperatures between 25-30°C for optimal germination. However, excessive heat or cold can inhibit germination, and the ideal temperature range should be maintained for optimal germination.

Plant hormone involvement

Plant hormones play a crucial role in the regulation of light requirements for germination. The hormones regulate several processes of seed development and growth, including seed dormancy, germination, and seedling establishment. The most important plant hormones involved in the regulation of germination are gibberellins, abscisic acid, and cytokinins.

Gibberellins

Gibberellins are plant hormones that promote seed germination, stem elongation, and flowering. They stimulate the synthesis of enzymes that hydrolyze stored food materials in the endosperm, such as amylase and protease. Gibberellins also promote the synthesis of α-amylase in the embryo, which breaks down starch in the endosperm to release glucose for energy. The activities of gibberellins are influenced by light, and they are most active under red and blue light.

Abscisic acid

Abscisic acid is a plant hormone that promotes seed dormancy and inhibits germination. It is produced in the embryos of mature seeds and inhibits the synthesis of growth-promoting hormones such as gibberellins. Abscisic acid also prevents seeds from germinating under unfavorable conditions, such as drought, low temperature, and lack of light. In the presence of light, abscisic acid is degraded, and its inhibitory effect on germination is reduced.

Cytokinins

Cytokinins are plant hormones that promote cell division and growth. They promote the growth of the radicle, which is the first part of the embryonic root to emerge from the seed coat during germination. Cytokinins also promote the synthesis of gibberellins and auxins, which are essential for stem elongation and cell differentiation. The activities of cytokinins are influenced by the duration and intensity of light, and they are most active under red light.

Light is a crucial factor influencing seed germination, and different species of plants have varying light requirements. Light affects seed dormancy, germination, and seedling establishment through its influence on photoreceptors, plant hormones, and plant growth regulators. The different colors of light, blue, and red, have different effects on plant growth and development, and their optimal intensity and duration depend on the species. Therefore, to optimize seed germination, growers must understand the light requirements for their crop species and provide the most suitable light conditions for optimal germination.

Chapter 32: Seed Scarification Techniques

Seed scarification is a process used to break, scratch, or soften the seed coat or testa for some species' seeds to allow for increased water uptake by the seed and promote germination. Seed scarification is especially important for seeds with hard seed coats or with an impermeable layer that prevents water from penetrating the seed's interior. Different techniques, such as mechanical, chemical, or biological methods, can be used for scarification, depending on the seed species. In this chapter, we will discuss the different scarification techniques, their advantages, and limitations.

Mechanical Scarification:

Mechanical scarification involves various physical processes that rupture the seed coat, allowing for water uptake. Mechanical scarification can be split into three categories: mechanical abrasion, scarifying through thermal shock, and manual scarification.

Mechanical Abrasion:

Mechanical abrasion is the most common method used for seed scarification. It involves the application of mechanical force to the seeds to wear down the seed coat. Some mechanical abrasion techniques include putting the seeds in a rock tumbler or rubbing the seeds against sandpaper or a metal file. However, care should be taken to ensure that the seed's embryo is not damaged when using these mechanical abrasion techniques.

Scarifying Through Thermal Shock:

Thermal shock involves exposing the seeds to fluctuating temperatures that cause rapid expansions and contractions of the seed coat, leading to its rupture. Seeds can be treated with warm water, followed by cold water, or they can be exposed to freezing temperatures, which cause the water inside the seed to freeze and expand, breaking the seed coat.

Manual Scarification:

Manual scarification involves using handheld tools such as a knife, scissors, or pliers to chip or nick the seed coat manually. Manual scarification is often used when dealing with smaller batches of seeds or when working with delicate seed types that cannot withstand mechanical or chemical treatments.

Chemical Scarification:

Chemical scarification involves using chemicals to erode or soften the seed coat, allowing water to penetrate the seed. However, care should be taken while using chemical scarification, as it can be dangerous to the user and the environment. Certain chemical scarification techniques include:

Sulphuric Acid:

Sulphuric acid scarification is a commonly used technique to scarify hard-coated seeds. Sulphuric acid destroys the seed coat's outer layer without damaging the seed's embryo. The seeds are immersed in concentrated sulphuric acid for a few minutes and then washed thoroughly with water. However, care should be taken when using sulphuric acid as it is a harmful chemical and is corrosive.

Hydrogen Peroxide:

Hydrogen peroxide is a relatively mild chemical scarification technique that can be used to soften seed coats. A low concentration of hydrogen peroxide can break down the seed coat while still being gentle enough to not damage the seed. Hydrogen peroxide can be applied to the seed by soaking it in a diluted solution for a few hours.

Potassium Nitrate:

Potassium nitrate is another excellent chemical scarification technique. When potassium nitrate comes in contact with water, it expands, causing pressure that can rupture the seed coat. Seeds are soaked in a potassium nitrate solution, which causes the seed coat to expand, allowing water to penetrate the seed.

Biological Scarification:

Biological scarification involves using living organisms that can break down the seed coat and stimulate germination by weakening the hardness, thickness, or impermeability of the seed coat. Different biological scarification techniques include:

Fungi:

Some species of fungi can break down the seed coat, allowing water to penetrate the seed. These fungi produce enzymes that can break down the organic matter in the seed coat. Seeds are soaked in water that is enriched with spores of fungi and left to incubate.

Animals:

Some animal species, such as rodents, can help break down seed coatings. When rodents eat the seeds, their digestive system can weaken the seed coat, promoting germination. Seeding habitats that depend on rodents for seed dispersal often produce seeds with specialized coatings.

Advantages and Limitations of Scarification Techniques:

Mechanical scarification is simple and does not require any equipment other than basic hand tools. It is also relatively inexpensive compared to chemical and biological scarification techniques. However, mechanical scarification may be ineffective or too damaging for some seed types.

Chemical scarification techniques yield great results and are reliable, but they present hazards to the environment, require safety precautions, and are costly. They also require careful disposal of chemicals used, as they can harm the environment.

Biological scarification is safe and natural, effective, and eco-friendly. However, it requires a longer time frame, and the conditions of the incubation must be well controlled.

Seed scarification is an essential process that can increase the germination success of some plant species. Mechanical, chemical, and biological scarification techniques can all be used to break down the seed coat, allowing for water uptake and promoting germination. Each scarification method brings its advantages and limitations, and some work better than others depending on the seed species. Careful attention is needed in selecting an appropriate scarification technique for seeds to increase germination success and protect the environment from harmful waste.

Chapter 33: Seed Stratification Techniques

Seed stratification is a process of treating seeds to convert them into viable seeds that can be sown. The stratification process involves exposing seeds to a specific set of environmental conditions that are required for the germination process to begin. This process is critical for the success of many types of plants, and it can be used to increase the germination rate of difficult-to-grow seeds.

There are different methods of seed stratification, and the specific technique used depends on the type of plant. The following methods can be used:

1. Cold Stratification

Cold stratification involves exposing seeds to cold temperatures for an extended period. This process simulates the winter conditions that seeds require to germinate, breaking down the seed coat, and allowing water and oxygen to enter the seed. The process can be done in a refrigerator or outdoors, depending on the climate and the plant being stratified.

It is essential to ensure the seeds do not freeze, as this can damage the seed. To prevent freezing, seeds can be placed into plastic bags with water and placed in a refrigerator. It is not necessary to add water to seeds that are not water absorbent.

Seeds that benefit from cold stratification include many varieties of trees, shrubs, and perennials. Cherry and apple trees, for example, require cold stratification to germinate successfully.

2. Warm Stratification

Warm stratification involves exposing seeds to warm temperatures for an extended period. This process stimulates the warm conditions required for germination in many types of plants. Warm stratification is typically used for seeds that have a hard seed coat.

Seeds can be placed in a sealed container and left in a warm location, or they can be chilled and then exposed to warm temperatures. Maintaining a warm, moist environment is critical for successful warm stratification.

Suitable seeds for warm stratification include sweet peas, petunias, and many types of annuals.

3. Scarification

Scarification is the mechanical or chemical process of breaking down seed coats to allow water and oxygen to enter the seed. This process simulates the natural process of seed coat breakdown in nature and can be done using different techniques depending on the seed type.

Mechanical scarification involves removing the seed coat using scissors, sandpaper, or a sharp blade. Chemical scarification involves treating the seed with acid or heat.

Seeds that benefit from scarification include lupines, morning glories, and many other types of perennials.

4. Smoke Stratification

Smoke stratification involves exposing seeds to smoke or smoke extracts to stimulate germination. This technique is common for many types of plants, particularly those native to Australia and Africa.

Smoke compounds increase the germination rate of seeds, as they are commonly found in the plant environment. Smoke stratification can be done using different techniques, including soaking seeds in smoke water or exposing the seeds to smoke from burning materials.

5. Darkness Stratification

Darkness stratification involves placing seeds in dark and cool conditions. This technique is used for seeds that require complete darkness to germinate or seeds that need a period of darkness to break the dormancy state.

The seeds should be kept moist, and the temperature should be consistent, to ensure successful germination. Seeds that benefit from darkness stratification include many types of wildflowers and perennials.

Seed stratification is an essential process to ensure the successful germination of seeds. The success of seed stratification depends on understanding the specific requirements of each plant type and applying the correct techniques. By selecting the right method, it is possible to germinate even the most challenging seeds.

Seed stratification is a critical process for many types of plants, and different techniques can be used for different seed types. By understanding the requirements of each plant and applying the correct technique, it is possible to increase the germination rate and grow a wider range of plants.

Chapter 34: Transplanting Seedlings

Transplanting seedlings is a crucial step in the gardening process, especially if you've started your plants indoors or in a greenhouse. It involves moving young plants from their original containers to a larger space, whether that's your garden or a larger pot. However, transplanting can be tricky if you're not careful. In this chapter, we'll cover why transplanting is necessary, when to do it, and how to do it successfully.

Why Transplant Seedlings?

Seedlings are typically started in small containers because they don't need a lot of space when they're first germinating. However, as they start to grow, they'll quickly outgrow their small home. If you keep them in a container that's too small, their roots will become bound and they will struggle to grow. When you transplant your seedlings, you'll give them room to stretch out their roots, which will help them grow into healthy, full-grown plants.

Another reason why transplanting is necessary is to space plants out. If you're growing multiple plants, you'll need to give them enough space to grow and avoid overcrowding. Overcrowding can lead to disease and stunted growth. By transplanting your seedlings, you can carefully space them out and give them the room they need to thrive.

When to Transplant Seedlings

Knowing when to transplant your seedlings is critical to their success. Transplanting too early or too late can be damaging to your plants. A good rule of thumb is to transplant when your plants have outgrown their current container or when they've grown to at least two inches tall with a few sets of true leaves.

One thing to keep in mind is to avoid transplanting during hot or dry weather. Seedlings are more susceptible to damage when they're stressed, and extreme heat or dryness can be particularly stressful. Wait until the weather has cooled down or choose a cool, cloudy day to give your plants the best chance of success.

Preparing for Transplanting

Before you start transplanting your seedlings, you'll need to make sure you have all the necessary equipment on hand. Here's a list of things you'll need:

- Larger Containers: You'll need a container that's at least two inches larger than your current container. Make sure the container has drainage holes at the bottom.
- Soil: Use a high-quality potting mix that's been specifically designed for growing plants in containers.
- Fertilizer: Seedlings need nutrients to grow, so consider adding a slow-release fertilizer to your potting mix.
- Water: Make sure you have a watering can or hose available to

water your plants.

- Labels: If you're growing multiple plants, label the containers with the plant name and date of transplanting.

Once you have everything you need, it's time to start preparing your seedlings for transplanting.

- Water your seedlings: Water your seedlings thoroughly the day before you plan to transplant them. Well-hydrated seedlings will be easier to transplant and will have a better chance of survival.
- Fill your larger container with soil: Fill your larger container with potting mix, leaving about one inch of space at the top.
- Dig a hole: Use a spoon or your fingers to dig a hole in the center of the container large enough to accommodate the root ball of your seedling.
- Gently tamp down soil: Gently tamp down the soil around the edges of the hole to prevent air pockets.
- Loosen the roots: Carefully remove the seedling from its current container. Gently loosen the roots if they appear to be root-bound. This will encourage the roots to grow outwards into the new soil.
- Plant the seedling: Plant the seedling in the center of the hole, making sure the soil level is the same as it was in the original container. Carefully fill in the hole with soil, making sure to tamp down the soil as you go.
- Water: Water your newly-transplanted seedling thoroughly, making sure the soil is saturated. You may also want to add a layer of mulch to help retain moisture.

Remember, transplanting can be a stressful experience for your seedlings. It's important to be gentle and avoid damaging the roots or stem while you're moving them to their new home. Once you've transplanted your seedlings, keep an eye on them and water them regularly to help them recover from the transplant shock.

Tips for Successful Transplanting

Transplanting seedlings may seem like a simple process, but there are a few things you can do to give your plants the best chance of success. Here are a few tips:

- Handle with care: Be gentle when handling your seedlings, especially the roots. Avoid pulling on the stem or leaves as this can damage the delicate tissues.
- Water well: Once you've transplanted your seedlings, water them well to help settle them in their new home. Keep the soil moist but not waterlogged to prevent root rot.
- Avoid over-fertilizing: While seedlings need nutrients to grow, too much fertilizer can be damaging. Stick with a slow-release fertilizer and avoid adding too much at once.
- Monitor for pests and disease: Transplanting can be a stressful time for your plants, which can make them more susceptible to pests and disease. Keep an eye out for any signs of problems and address them promptly.
- Don't transplant too early: Wait until your seedlings are large enough and the weather is favorable before transplanting.

Transplanting too early can cause damage and slow their growth.

Transplanting seedlings is an essential part of gardening that can help your plants grow into healthy, full-grown plants. By giving your seedlings enough space and nutrients to grow, you'll help them thrive and produce a bountiful harvest. While transplanting can be stressful for your seedlings, with a little care and attention, you can ensure they make the transition successfully.

Chapter 35: Dealing with Seedling Diseases

The emergence of seedling diseases in a farming system is quite common. It can be a result of a lack of knowledge, improper care taken during the planting period or harsh environmental conditions. Whatever the cause of the seedling disease may be, it is essential to detect and control the disease at the earliest stage possible. This book chapter aims to discuss the different types of seedling diseases, their potential risks, how to prevent them, and how to manage them effectively.

Types of Seedling Diseases

Seedling diseases are the diseases that impact the growth and development of young plants. These diseases can arise due to different factors such as environmental conditions, improper handling, and planting, soil-borne pathogens and seed-borne pathogens. Given below are the common types of seedling diseases that can occur in your farms:

1. Damping-Off

Damping-off is one of the most common diseases that affects seedlings. This disease is caused by several fungal pathogens, including Rhizoctonia spp, Phytium sp, and Fusarium spp. The disease usually affects the roots and the emerging shoots of the young seedlings, causing the plant to wilt and die.

2. Seedling Blight

Seedling blight can occur in seedlings that have already germinated. This disease is caused by fungal pathogens like Fusarium spp, Alternaria spp, and Rhizoctonia spp. Seedling blight can cause the young plants to turn brown and eventually die.

3. Root Rot

Root rot is a disease caused by different fungi species, including Pythium spp, Rhizoctonia spp, and Fusarium spp. The disease impacts the roots of the young seedlings, causing them to rot and decay. This, in turn, disrupts the plant's ability to absorb nutrients from the soil and can lead to stunted plant growth.

4. Leaf Spot

Leaf spot is a fungal disease that mainly affects the leaves of young plants. This disease can be caused by several different fungi species, including Alternaria spp and Cercospora spp. The disease usually causes the leaves to develop dark spots, which can eventually lead to defoliation of the plant.

5. Clubroot

Clubroot is a serious disease that affects members of the Brassicas family, including kale, broccoli, and cabbage. The disease is caused by the fungal pathogen Plasmodiophora brassicae. Clubroot can cause the roots of young seedlings to swell and form galls, leading to stunted plant growth and reduced yields.

Potential Risks of Seedling Diseases

Seedling diseases pose a significant risk to farmers' production and can lead to severe economic losses. This is because seedling diseases can impair the growth and development of young plants, leading to stunted growth, wilted plants, and eventually plant death. Some of the potential risks associated with seedling diseases include:

1. Reduced Yields

Seedling diseases can negatively impact a farmer's yield and revenue. This is because seedling diseases can reduce the overall stand that young plants have, leading to poor crop establishment and reduced yields.

2. Increased Farm Inputs

Farm inputs like fertilizers, pesticides, and herbicides are usually expensive. Seedling diseases can lead to an increase in these costs because farmers may need to apply these inputs more frequently to control the disease's spread.

3. Delayed Harvest

Seedling diseases can also lead to delayed harvests, especially if the farmer needs to replant or wait for new seedlings to be established before proceeding with the harvesting process. This can lead to a reduced income and slow down the farming operation.

Prevention of Seedling Diseases

Preventing seedling diseases is the best measure against the potential risks. Some of the ways to prevent seedling diseases include:

1. Use Quality Seeds

Using high-quality seeds is the first step to preventing seedling diseases. High-quality seeds are usually free from seed-borne pathogens and have a higher germination rate, leading to a healthier stand establishment.

2. Proper Sanitation

Proper sanitation measures can help prevent the spread of seedling diseases. This includes cleaning tools, equipment, and any other items that may have been in contact with infected plants.

3. Crop Rotation

Crop rotation is an excellent way to prevent seedling diseases. This helps to reduce the build-up of pathogens in the soil, preventing reoccurrence of disease among successive crops.

4. Proper Soil Management

Proper soil management, such as using organic matter, composting, and irrigation, can help maintain soil health and reduce the impact of soil-borne pathogens.

5. Environmental Management

Environmental factors, such as temperature, humidity, and sunlight, play a crucial role in plant growth and development. By controlling the environment, farmers can create conditions that are unfavorable for seedling diseases to thrive.

Managing Seedling Diseases

Managing seedling diseases is crucial to prevent loss of yield and revenue. Here are some of the ways to manage seedling diseases:

1. Chemical Control

Chemical control is an effective way of managing seedling diseases.

Fungicides can be applied to control pathogenic attacks on the young seedlings. However, the use of fungicides should be done in moderation to prevent the development of resistance to the chemicals.

2. Biological Control

Biological control involves using beneficial microorganisms to control seedling diseases. For example, fungal species like Trichoderma spp are known to produce enzymes that can break down the cell wall of fungal pathogens, reducing their impact on seedlings.

3. Cultural Controls

Cultural controls involve modifying cultivation practices and planting techniques to manage seedling diseases. For example, avoiding planting during cool and wet periods can prevent the development of damping-off. Late planting can also help to minimize the risk of clubroot infection.

4. Resistance Varieties

Planting disease-resistant varieties can prevent the spread and impact of seedling diseases. For example, some Brassica crop varieties have been bred with resistance to clubroot and other fungal pathogens.

Seedling diseases can be a significant threat to farmers' overall production and income. Preventing seedling diseases through proper sanitation measures, good soil management, and environmental control can help minimize the risk of seedling diseases. If an outbreak does occur, managing the disease through chemical control, biological control, and cultural controls can help to control the spread of the disease. By following the guidelines discussed in this chapter, farmers can minimize the risks of seedling diseases and improve their overall farm productivity.

Chapter 36: Troubleshooting Germination Problems

Growing plants from seeds can be extremely rewarding, but it isn't always a smooth process. Germination problems are common and can be frustrating for even the most experienced gardener. If you're struggling to get your seeds to germinate, don't worry - it's not uncommon. Here are some common problems you might encounter and some tips on how to troubleshoot them.

Problem: No Germination

If your seeds simply haven't sprouted, there are a few things that could be going wrong. Here are some things to consider:

- Temperature: Seeds generally need a specific temperature range to germinate. If the temperature is too high or too low, they might not germinate at all. Be sure to check the seed packet for information on the ideal temperature range for your seeds. If you're starting seeds indoors, be sure to keep the area where they're growing at the right temperature.

- Watering: Overwatering or underwatering can both be a problem when it comes to seed germination. If the soil is too wet, the seeds could rot before they have a chance to sprout. If the soil is too dry, they might not have enough moisture to sprout. It's important to keep the soil moist, but not waterlogged. Be sure to water consistently, but not too much at once.

- Soil Quality: If the soil isn't right, your seeds might not germinate. Be sure to use a good quality seed starting mix that's designed for starting seeds. This will help to ensure that the soil has the right texture, pH, and nutrients. If the soil is compacted or too heavy, it might be difficult for the seeds to sprout.

- Old Seeds: If your seeds are old, they might not germinate at all. Be sure to check the seed packet for an expiration date. If the seeds are more than a year or two old, they might not be viable.

Solution: Check to make sure that the soil temperature, watering, and soil quality are all within the ideal range for your seeds. If you suspect that your seeds might be old, try starting fresh with new seeds.

Problem: Slow Germination

If your seeds have sprouted, but they're taking a long time to do so, there are a few things that could be going on. Here are some things to consider:

- Temperature: Even if the temperature is within the ideal range for your seeds, it can still affect how quickly they germinate. If the temperature is too low, it might take longer for the seeds to sprout. Try raising the temperature slightly to see if it helps.

- Sunlight: If you're starting seeds indoors, they might not be getting enough sunlight to germinate quickly. Be sure to place them near a sunny window or use grow lights to provide enough light. If the seeds are outdoors, they might not be getting enough direct sunlight. Move them to a sunnier spot if possible.

- Seed Depth: If the seeds are planted too deep, it might take longer for them to reach the surface. Be sure to plant the seeds at the right depth - generally, only a quarter to half an inch deep.

Solution: Adjust the temperature or light conditions if necessary. Check the seed depth to make sure it's appropriate.

Problem: Uneven Germination

If some seeds have sprouted while others haven't, there are a few things that could be going on. Here are some things to consider:

- Uneven Watering: If the soil is too dry in some areas and too wet in others, it could affect how evenly the seeds germinate. Make sure to water consistently throughout the seed starting process.

- Inconsistent Temperature: If the temperature isn't consistent throughout the growing area, it could affect how evenly the seeds germinate. Be sure to check the temperature in different areas of the growing area to make sure it's consistent.

- Uneven Light: If the seeds aren't getting enough light, they might not germinate evenly. Make sure that they're getting enough direct light or adjust the placement of the grow lights to provide even coverage.

Solution: Make sure that the soil is consistently moist, check the temperature in different areas of the growing area to ensure it's consistent, and adjust the placement of grow lights if necessary.

Problem: Damping Off

Damping off is a common problem that occurs when seedlings rot or collapse at the soil line. It's caused by a fungus and can be a major problem for seed starting if not addressed promptly. Here's what you need to know:

- Prevention: The best way to prevent damping off is to keep the soil at the right moisture level and avoid overcrowding seedlings. Be sure to use a good quality seed starting mix and avoid overwatering.

- Treatment: If you notice signs of damping off, such as wilting or rotting seedlings, remove affected seedlings immediately. You can also try applying a fungicide to the soil to prevent further spread.

Solution: Prevention is key when it comes to damping off. Keep the soil at the right moisture level and avoid overcrowding seedlings to prevent it from occurring. If you notice signs of damping off, remove affected seedlings and consider applying a fungicide to prevent further damage.

Seed starting can be a fun and rewarding way to grow your own plants, but it can also be frustrating when things don't go as planned. If you're encountering germination problems, don't give up! By troubleshooting the problem and making the necessary adjustments, you can get your seeds to sprout and enjoy a successful harvest.

Chapter 37: Growing Plants from Seeds

Gardening can be a rewarding and enjoyable hobby that allows you to escape from the stresses of everyday life while being creative and providing fresh produce or vibrant flowers for your home. While many people prefer to purchase seedlings from a garden center, there is something special about growing a plant from seed. This chapter will explore the various aspects of growing plants from seeds, from selecting the right Seeds to nurturing them into healthy plants.

Selecting Seeds

When selecting seeds, it is important to consider the requirements of the plant, including its growing season, sun requirements, and hardiness. You should also consider the location where the plant will be grown, as some plants thrive in certain conditions while others require special care to flourish. It is important to choose seeds that are appropriate for your skill level and the time you have available to dedicate to your garden.

One way to ensure that you are selecting high-quality seeds is to choose from reputable suppliers. While it may be tempting to purchase cheaper seeds from discount stores, these seeds may not be as reliable or may not be suited to your garden's needs. To ensure the best results, purchase seeds from a reputable supplier who specializes in the type of plant you want to grow.

Preparing the Soil

Once you have selected your seeds, it is time to prepare the soil for planting. Soil preparation is critical to success, as the proper soil conditions can provide the nutrients the plant needs to thrive. Before planting, the soil should be rich in nutrients and have a pH level that is appropriate for the type of plant you are growing.

One way to determine the pH level of your soil is to test it with a soil test kit. These kits are inexpensive and are available at most gardening supply stores. The kit will provide you with a pH reading of your soil, which will allow you to adjust the soil's acidity or alkalinity to better match the needs of the plant.

Another important aspect of soil preparation is to ensure it is free of rocks or other debris that could impede the plant's growth. Before planting, clear the area of any rocks or debris, and add compost or other organic materials to the soil to enrich it with nutrients.

Planting Seeds

Once your soil is prepared, it is time to plant your seeds. The depth at which you should plant your seeds will depend on the type of plant you are growing, so be sure to read the seed packet's instructions carefully. In general, most seeds should be planted two to three times their diameter.

One common mistake people make when planting seeds is to plant them too deep. Seeds that are planted too deep may not receive enough oxygen, and may not germinate properly. If you are unsure of the correct planting depth, it is always better to err on the side of planting too shallow rather than too deep.

Another important consideration when planting seeds is spacing. Each type of plant has its own spacing requirements, which will vary according to its size and growth patterns. Be sure to space your seeds according to the instructions on the seed packet to ensure the best possible growth.

Watering Seeds

After planting, it is important to water your seeds regularly to keep the soil moist. However, be careful not to overwater, as this can cause the seeds to rot before they have a chance to germinate. In general, it is best to water the soil lightly every day or two, until the seeds have germinated and the plants have grown several inches tall.

Once the plants are established, you can begin to increase the amount of water you give them. Be sure to monitor the soil's moisture levels regularly, as overwatering can cause root rot and other problems with plant growth.

Lighting and Temperature

Lighting and temperature are critical factors in the success of growing plants from seeds. Most plants require lots of light to grow, so be sure to place your seeds in a location that receives ample sunlight throughout the day.

If you live in an area where there is not enough natural light, you may need to provide artificial light to help your plants grow. Grow lights are available at most gardening supply stores and can provide the right spectrum of light that your plants need to grow properly. In addition to lighting, temperature is also critical to seed germination and plant growth. Most plants require a specific temperature range for optimal growth, and it is important to ensure that your plants are not subjected to extreme temperature fluctuations.

During the day, plants should be kept in a location that receives ample sunlight and warmth. At night, it is important to move the plants into a cooler location to prevent them from becoming too warm. For best results, keep the temperature in your growing area at a consistent level to give your plants the best possible growing conditions.

Nurturing Your Plants

As your plants begin to grow, it is important to nurture them to ensure they remain healthy. This includes regular fertilization with the appropriate nutrients, pruning and trimming to encourage growth, and regular pest control to prevent damage from insects and other pests.

One of the easiest ways to provide your plants with the nutrients they need is to fertilize them regularly with an all-purpose fertilizer. These fertilizers are readily available at most gardening supply stores and can provide your plants with the nutrients they need to grow strong and healthy.

Pruning and trimming are important parts of plant care, as they encourage the growth of new shoots and leaves. Be sure to prune your plants regularly, removing any dead or damaged branches or leaves, to promote optimal growth.

Finally, regular pest control is critical to preventing damage from insects and other pests. Be sure to monitor your plants regularly for signs of disease or insect infestation, and treat them promptly to prevent further damage.

Growing plants from seeds is a rewarding and enjoyable hobby that can be enjoyed by people of all ages and skill levels. By choosing high-quality seeds, preparing the soil properly, and providing the right amount of light, water, and temperature, anyone can grow beautiful and healthy plants right in their own home. With a little patience and dedication, you can create a beautiful garden that will provide you with fresh produce and vibrant flowers year after year.

Chapter 38: Creating a Seed Starting Schedule

One of the most satisfying things about gardening is starting your own plants from seed. Not only does it save money, but it also gives you a greater sense of control over what you're growing. Starting from seed allows you to choose unique varieties that may not be readily available at your local garden center, and it lets you get a head start on the growing season by getting your plants started indoors before the weather is warm enough to plant outside.

But starting seeds can be a bit daunting, especially for beginners. There are lots of variables to consider, such as which seeds to plant, when to start them, how to care for them, and when to transplant them outdoors. By creating a seed starting schedule, you can take the guesswork out of the process and ensure that your plants have the best possible start.

Step 1: Determine your planting zone

The first step in creating a seed starting schedule is to determine your planting zone. This is important because it will determine when to start your seeds based on the date of your last expected frost. You can find your planting zone by visiting the USDA website and entering your zip code. Once you know your planting zone, you can use a seed starting chart to determine when to start your seeds.

Step 2: Choose your seeds

The next step is to choose which seeds you want to start. When choosing your seeds, consider what you want to grow and what is appropriate for your region and climate. Some good options for beginners include herbs, lettuce, tomatoes, and peppers, as they are easy to grow and relatively foolproof. Once you have decided which seeds you want to start, refer to the seed packets or a seed catalog for information on when to start them.

Step 3: Determine when to start your seeds

Now that you know your planting zone and which seeds you want to start, it's time to determine when to start them. Most seed packets will include information on when to start the seeds indoors, how long they take to germinate, and how many weeks before the last frost date they should be planted. Use this information to create a seed starting schedule.

For example, if you live in zone 6 and want to start tomatoes from seed, you would refer to the seed packet and see that they should be started indoors 6-8 weeks before the last frost date. You would then use a calendar to count back 6-8 weeks from your expected last frost date to determine when to start the seeds.

Step 4: Consider your growing conditions

In addition to your planting zone and the information on the seed packet, you also need to consider your growing conditions when creating a seed starting schedule. Some seeds may require more or less time to germinate or may need a specific temperature or amount of light. Make sure you read up on the specific requirements for each seed to ensure that you are providing the optimal conditions for germination and growth.

Step 5: Plan for transplanting

Finally, you need to plan for when to transplant your seedlings outdoors. This will depend on the type of plant and your growing conditions. Some plants, such as cold-hardy greens, can be planted outside as soon as the soil can be worked in the spring, while others, such as tomatoes, need to be acclimated to outdoor conditions before being planted.

In addition, you'll need to consider things like hardening off your seedlings and protecting them from pests and weather once they are planted. Make sure you research the specific needs of each plant to ensure that you are giving it the best chance of success.

Creating a seed starting schedule can seem overwhelming at first, but with a little planning and research, it can be a rewarding and enjoyable process. By taking the time to create a schedule, you can ensure that your plants have the best possible start and give yourself a head start on the growing season. Whether you're a novice or an experienced gardener, starting your own plants from seed is a great way to get the most out of your garden.

Chapter 39: Using Greenhouses for Seed Germination

The benefits of using greenhouses for seed germination are numerous, especially for gardeners who want to start their growing season early. Whether you're starting from seed or propagating cuttings, a greenhouse provides an environment that promotes healthy growth and reduces the risk of pests and disease. In this chapter, we will explore the various advantages of greenhouses for seed germination, the types of greenhouses available, and some tips on how to properly use them for optimal results.

Advantages of Greenhouses for Seed Germination

1. Controlled Environment

One of the most significant benefits of using a greenhouse for seed germination is that you can control the environment in which your seeds grow. With precise control over temperature, humidity, and light levels, you can create the ideal growing conditions for your plants. This means that you can start your seeds earlier in the year, without worrying about frost or other weather conditions that could damage or kill your young plants.

2. Fewer Pests and Diseases

Using a greenhouse for seed germination also reduces the risk of pests and diseases. Because greenhouses are enclosed structures, they prevent pests from getting to your plants, and they also provide a barrier against diseases that can be transmitted through soil or water. This means that your plants are less likely to suffer from common garden problems like aphids, cutworms, and fungal diseases.

3. Faster Growth

Another benefit of using a greenhouse for seed germination is that your plants will grow faster. This is because the controlled environment inside a greenhouse provides all of the essential nutrients, water, and light that your plants need to grow quickly and healthily. This means that you can harvest your vegetables or flowers earlier in the season and enjoy the fruits of your labor sooner.

Types of Greenhouses

There are several types of greenhouses available, each with its own advantages and disadvantages. The type of greenhouse that you choose will depend on your needs, budget, and the size of your garden. Here are some of the most common types of greenhouses:

1. Lean-to greenhouses

Lean-to greenhouses are attached to the side of a house or other structure. They are typically smaller than other types of greenhouses and are designed to take advantage of the warmth and light generated by the sun.

2. Quonset greenhouses

Quonset greenhouses are made of arched metal frames that are covered with plastic or polycarbonate panels. They are typically low-cost and easy to assemble, making them a popular choice for gardeners on a budget.

3. Gable greenhouses

Gable greenhouses are freestanding structures that have peaked roofs. They are typically larger than other types of greenhouses and are designed to provide ample space for growing a variety of plants.

4. Dome greenhouses

Dome greenhouses are unique in their design and are typically used for growing exotic or tropical plants that require specialized growing conditions. They are typically made of fiberglass or polycarbonate panels and are more expensive than other types of greenhouses.

Tips for Using Greenhouses for Seed Germination

1. Plan Your Layout

Before you start germinating your seeds in a greenhouse, you should plan your layout carefully. This means deciding on the type of greenhouse that you want, the size of your growing area, and the types of plants that you want to grow. You should also consider the amount of space that you have available, as well as the type of soil and sun exposure in your garden.

2. Choose the Right Seeds

Choosing the right seeds is essential for successful seed germination. You should choose seeds that are well-suited to your garden's soil and growing conditions, as well as your climate. You can find this information on the packaging of your seeds or by researching them online.

3. Temperature Control

Controlling the temperature in your greenhouse is crucial for successful seed germination. Most seeds need temperatures between 60 and 85 degrees Fahrenheit to germinate properly. You can maintain the optimal temperature by using a heat mat or a space heater, as well as by opening or closing vents to adjust airflow.

4. Watering

Watering your plants properly is also essential for successful seed germination. You should water your seeds regularly, but not too much. Overwatering can lead to root rot and other problems. You can water your seeds by misting them or by using a watering can with a fine nozzle.

5. Light

Providing your plants with enough light is also essential for successful seed germination. Most plants need between 12 and 14 hours of light per day to grow properly. You can provide this light by using fluorescent or LED grow lights, as well as by making sure that your greenhouse receives plenty of natural sunlight.

Using greenhouses for seed germination can provide numerous benefits to gardeners who want to start their growing season early. With a controlled environment, fewer pests and diseases, and faster growth, a greenhouse is an essential tool for successful seed germination. By choosing the right type of greenhouse, carefully planning your layout, and following proper seed germination techniques, you can enjoy a bountiful harvest of vegetables or flowers all season long.

Chapter 40: Direct Sowing vs. Starting Indoors

Growing your own garden can be an incredibly satisfying and rewarding experience. Whether you're growing vegetables for a sustainable lifestyle, flowers for aesthetic appeal, or a combination of both, there are a few important choices to make before getting started. One of the biggest decisions is whether to direct sow or start your seeds indoors. Both methods have their advantages and disadvantages, and your decision will depend on a variety of factors.

Direct Sowing

Direct sowing is the process of planting your seeds directly into the soil where you want them to grow. This is most commonly done outdoors in a garden bed or container, but can also be done in a greenhouse or other protected environment.

Advantages

One of the biggest advantages of direct sowing is the simplicity and convenience. You don't need any special equipment or supplies, and you don't have to worry about transplanting your seedlings. Simply choose your location, prepare your soil, and sow your seeds. Direct sowing is also a great way to save time and effort, as you'll bypass the need to transplant your seedlings.

Direct sowing is also advantageous for plants that don't transplant well, such as root vegetables like carrots, potatoes, and onions. These plants have sensitive roots that can easily become damaged during transplanting, which can hinder their growth and development.

Another benefit of direct sowing is that it can help create a more natural environment for your plants. When seeds are sown directly into the soil, they grow in the same environment they will spend their entire life in. This can make them hardier and better adapted to their surroundings.

Disadvantages

While direct sowing can be simple and convenient, it's not always the best choice for every plant or situation. One of the main disadvantages of direct sowing is that it can result in lower germination rates. Seeds that are sown directly into the soil are exposed to the elements, meaning they may not receive the optimal conditions for germination. Factors like temperature, moisture, and sunlight can all impact germination rates, and it's not always possible to control these factors.

Direct sowing can also be risky if you're planting in an area with a lot of pests or diseases. Plants that are grown from direct seed can be more susceptible to pests and disease, as they may not have the same level of protection as transplants grown indoors.

Starting Indoors

Starting your seeds indoors is the process of growing your seeds in containers or trays indoors before transplanting them outdoors. This method is commonly used for starting vegetable and flower gardens. Starting seeds indoors allows you to germinate your seeds in a protected environment, where you can closely monitor and control the conditions for optimal growth.

Advantages

One of the biggest advantages of starting seeds indoors is the ability to control the growing environment. When you start seeds indoors, you can control the temperature, humidity, light, and soil conditions to provide your seedlings with the optimal environment for growth. This can result in higher germination rates, stronger plants, and a better overall yield.

Starting seeds indoors is also advantageous for plants that have a long growing season or require warmer temperatures to germinate. This method allows you to get a head start on the growing season, providing your plants with a longer time to mature before the first frost.

Starting seeds indoors can also be advantageous for plants that require a lot of maintenance or care. This method allows you to closely monitor the growth and development of your plants, allowing you to quickly address any issues or problems that arise.

Disadvantages

While starting seeds indoors can be advantageous, it's not always the best choice for every plant or situation. One of the main disadvantages of starting seeds indoors is the cost and time commitment. Starting seeds indoors requires more equipment and supplies, including trays, pots, soil mix, and grow lights. It also requires more time and attention, as you'll need to monitor and care for your seedlings regularly.

Another disadvantage of starting seeds indoors is the need for transplanting. Once your seedlings have reached a certain size, they'll need to be transplanted outdoors. Transplanting can be stressful for plants, and it can be difficult to replicate the same growing conditions they experienced indoors. This can result in a slower growth rate and weaker plants.

Which Method is Right for You?

Deciding whether to direct sow or start your seeds indoors will depend on a variety of factors, including the type of plants you want to grow, the climate and growing conditions in your area, and your personal preferences and experience.

If you're new to gardening or want to keep things simple and low-cost, direct sowing may be the best choice for you. Direct sowing is also a great option if you're growing plants that don't transplant well or if you want to create a more natural environment for your plants.

If you're an experienced gardener or want to maximize your yield and plant health, starting your seeds indoors may be the best choice for you. Starting seeds indoors allows for more control over the growing environment, providing your plants with the optimal conditions for growth and development. This method is also great for plants with long growing seasons or that require more care and attention.

Direct sowing and starting seeds indoors are both viable options for growing a garden, and each method has its own advantages and disadvantages. Ultimately, the decision of which method to choose will depend on your goals, preferences, and experience level. Whether you choose to direct sow or start your seeds indoors, the most important thing is to give your plants the care and attention they need to thrive and produce a bountiful harvest.

Chapter 41: Composting for Seed Starting

Composting is a process of converting organic waste into a nutrient-rich soil amendment that gardeners use to increase the health and productivity of their plants. Compost contains microorganisms that break down the organic matter, creating a soil-like substance that is rich in nutrients and beneficial to plants. Gardeners have long appreciated the benefits of using compost in their gardens, but some are unaware that it is also excellent for starting seeds.

The benefits of composting

Composting has several benefits for both the environment and the gardener. First, it reduces the amount of organic waste that ends up in landfills. Organic waste makes up a significant portion of household waste, and when it is sent to landfills, it decomposes anaerobically, producing methane, a potent greenhouse gas. By composting, gardeners reduce the amount of waste they send to landfills, which can help reduce greenhouse gas emissions.

Composting also improves soil health. The microorganisms in compost break down the organic matter, releasing nutrients that plants need to grow. Compost contains nitrogen, phosphorus, and potassium, the three primary macronutrients that plants require. It also contains micronutrients like calcium, magnesium, and sulfur, which are necessary for plant growth but needed in smaller amounts.

Moreover, compost loosens clay soils, making them more porous and better draining. In contrast, it adds structure to sandy soils, improving their water-holding capacity. Compost also increases the soil's ability to retain nutrients and reduces the need for chemical fertilizers, which can be harmful to the environment.

The benefits of using compost for seed starting

Starting seeds is an essential part of gardening, and using compost can improve the success rate of seedlings. Compost provides several key benefits for seed starting:

Better soil structure: Compost improves the physical structure of soil, making it easier for seedling roots to penetrate and establish themselves.

More nutrients: Compost contains a wide range of nutrients that young seedlings need to grow. These nutrients are available in a form that plants can easily absorb.

Improved water-holding capacity: Compost improves the soil's ability to hold water, which is critical for healthy seedling growth.

Increases microbial activity: Compost contains microorganisms that help decompose organic matter and break down nutrients into a form plants can use. These microorganisms can help prevent disease in young seedlings.

Less dependence on synthetic fertilizers: Compost provides a rich source of nutrients, reducing the need for synthetic fertilizers that can be harmful to the environment.

Steps to making compost for seed starting

To use compost for seed starting, gardeners must create a compost that is suitable for seedlings. Here are the steps to making compost for seed starting:

Step 1: Collect organic matter

The first step in making compost is to collect organic matter. Gardeners can use a wide variety of materials, including kitchen scraps, yard waste, and animal manure. Suitable materials for a compost heap used for seed starting include:

Fruit and vegetable scraps

Coffee grounds and filters

Tea bags

Eggshells

Grass clippings

205

Leaves

Twigs and branches

Animal manure

Step 2: Create a compost bin

Once gardeners have collected enough organic matter, they need to create a compost bin. There are many ways to do this, from purchasing a commercial compost bin to making one using reclaimed materials. A compost bin should be large enough to accommodate the amount of organic matter being composted and should be aerated to allow air to circulate.

Step 3: Add organic matter to the bin

The next step is to add the organic matter to the compost bin. Gardeners should layer the materials, starting with a layer of brown material like leaves, followed by a layer of green material like vegetable scraps. They should continue layering the materials until the bin is full, being careful not to add too much of any one material.

Step 4: Keep the compost moist

Moisture is essential for composting, and gardeners should keep the compost moist but not soaking wet. Ideally, the compost should have the consistency of a wrung-out sponge. If it is too dry, it will take longer to decompose. If it is too wet, it may become anaerobic and start to smell.

Step 5: Turn the compost

Finally, gardeners should turn the compost every one to two weeks to aerate it. This helps break down the organic matter faster and ensures that the compost is evenly decomposed. Turning the compost also helps prevent odors and ensures that the compost is ready when it is needed for seed starting.

Using compost for seed starting

Once gardeners have created compost, they can use it to start seeds. Here are the steps to using compost for seed starting:

Step 1: Fill seed-starting containers with compost

The first step is to fill seed-starting containers with compost. Gardeners can use anything from recycled egg cartons to commercial seed-starting trays. They should fill the containers to within a half-inch of the top.

Step 2: Plant the seeds

Next, gardeners should plant the seeds according to the package instructions. When planting seeds in compost, gardeners should make sure to plant them at the right depth. Most seeds should be planted at a depth of two to three times their diameter, but some require shallower planting.

Step 3: Water the seeds

After planting the seeds, gardeners should water the compost thoroughly. It is essential to keep the compost moist but not soaking wet. Gardeners should check the compost daily and water as needed.

Step 4: Provide light and warmth

Finally, gardeners should provide light and warmth for the seedlings. Most seeds require a temperature of around 70 degrees Fahrenheit to germinate, so gardeners may need to provide a heat source. Once the seedlings have germinated, they will require six to eight hours of direct sunlight each day.

Composting for seed starting is an excellent way to improve soil health and give seedlings a healthy start. By using compost, gardeners can provide young plants with the nutrients they need to thrive while reducing their dependence on synthetic fertilizers. Composting is also good for the environment, reducing greenhouse gas emissions and producing a valuable soil amendment that reduces the amount of organic waste sent to landfills. Whether starting seeds indoors or outdoors, using compost is a smart, sustainable gardening practice that benefits all.

Chapter 42: Organic Seed Saving Practices

Organic Seed Saving Practices

Saving seeds is one of the most important practices in agriculture, which not only helps farmers save money, but also helps maintain biodiversity in crops. Organic seed saving practices, in particular, are those that promote the use of natural methods of farming that do not involve the use of chemical pesticides and fertilizers. These practices make use of the natural traits of crops to protect against pests and disease, improve soil fertility, and enhance crop yields.

In this chapter, we will discuss the most common organic seed saving practices that farmers use to preserve crop diversity and maintain the health of their crops. These practices include selecting healthy and robust seed varieties, harvesting and cleaning seeds properly, storing seeds in appropriate conditions, and exchanging seeds with other farmers and seed banks.

Selecting Healthy and Robust Seeds

Farmers who practice organic seed saving must start by selecting the most healthy and robust seeds from their crops. This helps ensure that the seed varieties they save will be strong enough to maintain biodiversity and adapt to changing environmental conditions. To select the best seeds, farmers need to:

- Observe the plants: Farmers should observe the plants in their fields throughout the growing season, looking for traits like quick flowering, strong roots, and high yielding.

- Test the seeds: Before harvesting, farmers should test the seeds, checking that they are mature and healthy enough to store. This can be done by inspecting the seeds for visual characteristics such as discoloration or visible damage.

- Choose the best seeds: Farmers should choose the best seeds from the crops and avoid using seeds from any plants with poor yields or that display unhealthy traits.

Harvesting and Cleaning Seeds Properly

The next step in organic seed saving is to harvest and clean the seeds properly. Harvesting the seeds at the right time is critical to maintaining their health and viability. Once the seeds are harvested, they must be cleaned to remove any debris, such as bits of plants, insects, or dirt. To harvest and clean seeds properly, farmers need to:

- Harvest at the right time: The timing of seed harvesting varies depending on the crop and its location. Farmers need to consider factors such as when the seeds are mature and when the weather is dry enough to prevent spoilage.

- Dry the Seeds: Drying the seeds in a cool and dry place ensures that they are not exposed to moisture. After harvesting seeds, farmers should spread them out in a single layer shade in a well-ventilated area.

- Clean the Seeds: Once the seeds are dry, farmers can thresh them, resulting in clean seeds without unwanted debris or plant material. Small seeds can be separated by sifting them through a fine mesh, and larger seeds can be gently tapped or shaken to eliminate dirt or dust.

Storing Seeds in Appropriate Conditions

Storing seeds in appropriate conditions is crucial to maintaining their viability and longevity. Proper storage conditions are cool, dry, and oxygen-free environments. The temperature range should be between 32°F and 41°F, with humidity levels of less than 50%. Seed viability diminishes over time, and to keep the seeds viable for many years, they must be stored in suitable seed containers like glass jars or sealed plastic containers. To store seeds properly, farmers need to:

- Choose a suitable storage container: Glass jars or plastic bags with a zipper seal work best for seed storage.

- Label the storage container: Label the container with the name, type of seed, and date of collection to avoid confusion.

- Store seeds at a cool temperature: Store the seeds in a place where the temperature is between 32°F and 41°F. If such conditions are unlikely to be found, seeds can be stored in a refrigerator or a freezer.

Exchanging Seeds with Other Farmers and Seed Banks

Organic seed saving also involves exchanging seeds with other farmers and seed banks. Seed exchange programs facilitate the sharing of seed varieties among farmers, helping to preserve crop diversity. Farmers can exchange seeds with one another or through seed banks. Seed banks collect and store seeds from different varieties of plants, protecting them from extinction. Farmers can also exchange seeds online through various websites.

In conclusion, organic seed saving practice is an essential aspect of farming that requires attention and adherence to the right methods. Farmers must choose healthy and robust seeds, harvest and clean them properly, store them under suitable conditions, and exchange them with other farmers and seed banks. By following these practices, farmers can maintain biodiversity in their crops, improve soil fertility and protect against crop diseases, all while contributing to the overall health of the environment.

Chapter 43: Saving Seeds from Perennial Plants

Perennial plants are those that grow for more than two years, and many of these plants have seeds that can be saved and used to grow new plants. This practice of saving seeds has been used for many years by gardeners, farmers, and seed collectors, and it's a great way to ensure a steady supply of plants for the future.

In order to save seeds from perennial plants, there are a few things that need to be taken into consideration. First, it's important to understand the different types of seeds that are produced by these plants. There are two types of seeds, open-pollinated and hybrid seeds. Open-pollinated seeds are those that have been pollinated naturally, by insects or wind, for example. Hybrid seeds, on the other hand, are the result of cross-pollination between two different plant species or varieties.

If you're interested in saving seeds from perennial plants, it's generally best to stick with open-pollinated seeds. This is because they are more likely to produce plants that are similar to their parent plants, whereas hybrid seeds can produce unpredictable results.

When it comes to selecting plants to save seeds from, there are a few things to keep in mind. First, it's important to choose plants that are healthy and disease-free. Additionally, it's best to choose plants that have produced a large number of fruits or flowers, as this indicates good fertility and a higher chance of producing viable seeds.

Once you've selected your plants, it's time to start harvesting the seeds. The exact process will vary depending on the type of plant you're working with, but here are some general guidelines to follow:

1. Wait until the seeds are mature. Before you start harvesting seeds, it's important to wait until they are fully mature. This will vary depending on the plant species, but in general, seeds should be left on the plant until they have changed color and become dry and hard.

2. Remove the seeds from the plant. Once the seeds are mature, you'll need to remove them from the plant. This can typically be done by gently shaking the seed pods or flowers over a container, or by cutting off the seed heads and collecting the seeds manually.

3. Dry the seeds. After you've harvested the seeds, it's important to dry them out thoroughly. This can be done by laying them out in a single layer on a tray or piece of paper, and leaving them in a well-ventilated area for several days. Once the seeds are completely dry, they can be stored in an airtight container.

4. Label and store the seeds. Before you store your seeds, it's important to label them with the plant species, the date they were harvested, and any other relevant information. This will make it easier to keep track of your seeds over time. Once the seeds are labeled, they can be stored in a cool, dark place until you're ready to use them.

In addition to following these general guidelines, there are a few specific things to keep in mind when saving seeds from certain types of perennial plants. Here's a closer look at some of the most common types of perennial plants, and how to save seeds from them:

Herbs

Herbs are a popular type of perennial plant that can be easily grown in a home garden. Many herbs also produce seeds that can be saved and used for future plantings. Here's how to save seeds from some of the most popular herbs:

• Basil: To save basil seeds, wait until the flowers have turned brown and the seeds are fully formed. Cut off the seed heads and place them in a paper bag. Shake the bag gently to remove the seeds.

• Dill: Dill produces seeds that are commonly used in cooking. To harvest dill seeds, wait until the flowers have turned brown and the seeds are fully mature. Cut off the seed heads and place them in a paper bag. Shake the bag gently to remove the seeds.

• Mint: Mint can be grown from seeds, but it's much easier to propagate mint plants from cuttings. However, if you do want to save mint seeds, wait until the flowers have turned brown and the seeds are fully mature. Cut off the seed heads and place them in a paper bag. Shake the bag gently to remove the seeds.

• Thyme: Thyme produces small, brown seeds that can be saved and used for future plantings. Wait until the flowers have turned brown and the seeds are fully mature, then cut off the seed heads and place them in a paper bag. Shake the bag gently to remove the seeds.

Perennial Flowers

Perennial flowers are another popular type of plant that can be easily grown in a home garden. Here's how to save seeds from some of the most common types of perennial flowers:

• Coneflowers: To save coneflower seeds, wait until the seed heads have turned brown and the seeds are fully mature. Cut off the seed heads and place them in a paper bag. Shake the bag gently to remove the seeds.

• Daylilies: Daylilies produce seeds inside their seed pods, which can be harvested once they turn brown and start to crack open. Cut off the seed pods and allow them to dry out thoroughly before removing the seeds.

• Irises: To save iris seeds, wait until the seed pods have turned brown and dried out. Cut off the seed pods and allow them to dry out further before removing the seeds.

• Peonies: Peonies produce large, round seed pods that can be harvested once they turn yellow and start to split open. Cut off the seed pods and allow them to dry out thoroughly before removing the seeds.

Fruit Trees

Fruit trees are a bit more complex when it comes to saving seeds, as many of them require a process called stratification in order to germinate properly. Here's how to save seeds from some of the most common types of fruit trees:

• Apples: To save apple seeds, wait until the apples have fully ripened and the seeds are brown and mature. Remove the seeds from the core of the apple and dry them out thoroughly. Once the seeds are dry, they will need to be stratified before planting.

• Cherries: To save cherry seeds, remove the seeds from the fruit and allow them to dry out thoroughly. Once the seeds are dry, they will need to be stratified before planting.

• Plums: To save plum seeds, remove the seeds from the fruit and allow them to dry out thoroughly. Once the seeds are dry, they will need to be stratified before planting.

• Peaches: To save peach seeds, remove the seeds from the fruit and allow them to dry out thoroughly. Once the seeds are dry, they will need to be stratified before planting.

Saving seeds from perennial plants is a great way to ensure a steady supply of plants for future gardens. By following these guidelines and tips, you can successfully harvest and store seeds from a wide variety of plants, from herbs to fruit trees. Whether you're an experienced gardener or just getting started, seed-saving is a valuable skill to have, and one that will serve you well for years to come.

Chapter 44: Saving Seeds from Annual Plants

Annual plants are those that complete their entire life cycle within one year. They germinate, grow, flower, set seed, and die all within that one period. Some examples of common annual plants include zinnia, marigold, corn, and beans. If you are a gardener who loves to grow annual plants, then you might want to learn how to save the seeds from your favorite plants. Saving annual plant seeds is not difficult, but it's important to do it correctly to ensure that your seeds will grow successfully in the next growing season.

Why Save Seeds from Annual Plants?

There are many good reasons to save seeds from your annual plants. One of the most important reasons is that it allows you to perpetuate your favorite plants for future growing seasons. If you have a particular variety of zinnia, for example, that you really love, saving the seeds will allow you to grow that same variety next year. This is especially important if the variety is rare or hard to find.

Another reason to save seeds is that it can save you money in the long run. Instead of having to buy new seed packets every year, you can simply save the seeds from your existing plants and use them to grow new plants.

Lastly, saving seeds from your annual plants can provide you with a deeper understanding of the life cycle of plants. By observing the process of seed development and harvesting, you can gain insight into the intricacies of plant reproduction and the science of genetics.

Which Plants are Best to Save Seeds From?

Although it's technically possible to save seeds from any annual plant, some plants are easier to save seeds from than others. Generally, the best plants to save seeds from are those that are open-pollinated (meaning they are pollinated by insects or wind, rather than being cross-pollinated by human intervention) and those that produce large quantities of seeds.

Some examples of plants that are easy to save seeds from include beans, peas, lettuce, marigolds, zinnias, and sunflowers. Corn is also relatively easy to save seeds from, but it requires a bit more effort and knowledge because it is wind-pollinated, which can lead to cross-pollination with other nearby corn plants.

How to Save Seeds from Annual Plants

Saving seeds from annual plants is not difficult, but it does require some basic knowledge and a bit of patience. Here are the steps to follow:

Step 1: Allow the seed pods to mature

To have the best chance of saving viable seeds, it's important to allow the seed pods to fully mature on the plant. This means waiting until the flower petals have fallen off and the seed pod has dried out and turned brown. For example, if you are saving seeds from a marigold plant, you'll want to wait until the flower petals have yellowed and fallen off and the seed pod has turned brown and dried out.

Step 2: Remove the seed pods from the plant

Once the seed pods have matured, remove them from the plant. You can do this by gently pulling on the stem or by cutting the stem with a pair of clean scissors or pruning shears. Be sure to collect the seed pods in a paper bag or envelope so that you don't lose any of the seeds.

Step 3: Break open the seed pods

Once you've collected the seed pods, it's time to extract the seeds. Depending on the plant, the seeds may be either inside the seed pod or attached to it on the outside. For example, with beans or peas, the seeds are inside the pod, while with marigolds or zinnias, the seeds are attached to the outside of the pod.
To extract the seeds, you'll need to break open the seed pods. You can do this by gently crushing the pods with your fingers or by using a small tool like a pair of pliers or a nutcracker. Be careful not to crush the seeds themselves.
Step 4: Clean the seeds

Once the seeds have been extracted from the seed pods, they will likely be covered in chaff and other debris. To clean the seeds, you can either use your hands or a small strainer. Simply rub the seeds between your palms or shake them gently in the strainer to remove any extraneous material.

Step 5: Allow the seeds to dry

After the seeds have been cleaned, allow them to dry completely before storing them. This will help prevent mold and other problems. To dry the seeds, place them on a clean, dry surface like a plate or baking sheet and leave them in a warm, dry place for several days. Be sure to stir the seeds occasionally to ensure that they dry evenly.

Step 6: Store the seeds

Once the seeds are completely dry, you can store them in airtight containers like glass jars or plastic bags. Be sure to label the containers with the plant name and the date of harvest so that you know what's inside and how old the seeds are. Store the containers in a cool, dry place like a pantry or basement.

Saving seeds from your annual plants is a fun and rewarding activity for gardeners. With a bit of knowledge and some patience, you can successfully save seeds from your favorite plants and ensure that they will grow successfully in the next growing season. Whether you're looking to perpetuate a rare variety or simply save money, saving seeds from your annual plants is a great way to deepen your understanding of the life cycle of plants and the science of genetics.

Chapter 45: Seed Saving from Biennial Plants

For many gardeners, saving seeds from plants is a time-honored tradition. By preserving the seeds of favorite plants, gardeners can cultivate plants that are well suited to their individual growing environment, and often with a better overall performance than new hybrid varieties. Biennial plants are a popular choice for seed saving, as they possess a unique life cycle that allows for the best seed harvest. In this chapter, we will explore the methods for seed saving from biennial plants.

Understanding Biennial Plants

To begin, it is important to understand what biennial plants are. Biennial plants are those that complete their life cycle in two years. In the first year, the plant grows leaves and a root system, storing energy in the form of carbohydrates. In the second year, the plant will produce flowers, fruit, and seeds. Once the plant has completed its life cycle, it dies, making biennial plants a useful plant for seed saving. Common examples of biennial plants include carrots, beets, parsnips, leeks, and many varieties of herbs.

Choosing Biennial Plants for Seed Saving

When selecting biennial plants for seed saving, it is important to choose those that are suited to your growing environment. Plants that thrive in your climate are more likely to produce healthy and viable seed. Choose plants that have shown good resistance to pests and disease, and those that have produced reliable and robust crops in the past.

Harvesting Biennial Plant Seeds

The key to a successful seed harvest from biennial plants is timing. Seeds should be harvested when they are fully ripe, but before they fall from the plant. The best way to do this is to closely monitor the plant as it goes through its second year. Once the plant has produced flowers, it will begin to produce seed heads. These heads will become increasingly dry as they mature. Once the seed heads have completely dried out, it is time to harvest the seeds. This is the stage when the seeds are at their most viable.

To harvest the seed heads, use clean and sharp garden scissors or pruning shears. Cut the heads off the plant, making sure to keep the dried flower heads intact. Next, carefully strip the seeds from the seed heads, being sure to remove any chaff or debris. Place the seeds into a paper bag or an envelope, and label with the type of plant and the date of harvest.

Seed Storage

Once the seeds have been harvested, it is important to store them in a cool, dry place until they are ready to be planted. Biennial plant seeds can be stored for several years, making them an ideal choice for gardeners who want to ensure a continuous supply of their favorite plants. When storing seeds, it is important to keep them away from moisture, light, and pests. A cool, dark place like a basement or root cellar is ideal.

Planting Biennial Plant Seeds

When it comes time to plant your biennial plant seeds, there are a few important steps to follow to ensure a successful harvest. Begin by preparing the soil where you will be planting the seeds. Choose a location that receives full sun and has well-draining soil. Remove any rocks and debris from the soil, and mix in compost or fertilizer to help improve soil quality.

Next, plant the seeds at the appropriate depth for the type of plant. Be sure to follow the instructions on the seed packet to ensure proper planting. Once the seeds are in the ground, water them well and cover them with a layer of mulch to help retain moisture in the soil.

Caring for Biennial Plants

As the biennial plant grows, it is important to provide it with the care it needs to thrive. Depending on the variety of plant, this may include regular watering, pruning, and pest control. Be sure to monitor the plant carefully, and address any problems that may arise promptly. This will help ensure a healthy plant and a bountiful harvest of seeds.

Saving biennial plant seeds is a great way to ensure a continuous supply of your favorite plants year after year. By choosing plants that are well suited to your growing environment and carefully harvesting and storing the seeds, you can produce robust and healthy crops for years to come. Whether you are a seasoned gardener or just starting out, seed saving from biennial plants is a rewarding and satisfying way to enjoy the beauty and bounty of your own garden.

Chapter 46: Climate Considerations for Seed Saving

We are living in an era where environmental changes are a reality, and one of the most significant challenges that individuals face today is seed saving. Although seed-saving is not a new thing, this ancient agricultural practice is becoming a critical skill to have in these modern times when seeds' availability is decreasing. As a result, gardeners, farmers, and environmentalists are turning to seed saving as a way of preserving and perpetuating plants, promoting biodiversity, and adapting to climate change. It is vital to consider the climatic conditions when it comes to saving seeds, as these variables play an important role in determining the success of seed saving. This chapter explores some of the climate-related factors to consider when saving seeds.

Understanding Climatic Conditions

Climatic conditions are how the atmosphere behaves over a long period of time. These conditions include temperature, rainfall, humidity, wind, and solar radiation. Climatic conditions are especially important when determining the optimal growing conditions for plants. By understanding climatic conditions, gardeners and farmers can determine which plants are suitable for a specific location and the time when the plant will grow best. Similarly, it is important to understand the climatic needs of plants when it comes to seed saving.

Temperature

The temperature influences many aspects of seed saving, including seed viability, seed dormancy, and seed storage. Seeds are living organisms, and they require a specific range of temperature to germinate successfully. Every plant species has a specific temperature range that is optimal for germination, and it is important to understand these requirements when planning to save seed.

High temperatures can decrease seed viability and reduce the germination rate. At the same time, low temperatures can also affect the germination of some seeds, especially in frost-prone areas. Thus, it is essential to know the optimal temperature range for your specific seeds, both during their growing and storage stages. For example, seeds of cool-season crops like broccoli, lettuce, and radishes require cool temperatures for germination and growth. On the other hand, warm-season crops like tomatoes and peppers require warmer temperatures.

Rainfall

Rainfall influences seed saving in several ways. Excessive rainfall can cause seeds to rot, while low rainfall can cause seeds to become desiccated or dry out completely. Therefore, assessing rainfall patterns is essential when saving seeds. Knowing when to plant, harvest, and dry seeds is important when considering rainfall. In general, when seeds mature during the rainy season, it is essential to remove them from the plant and dry them immediately. During the dry season, it is important to water the plants regularly to ensure that the seeds do not become too dry.

Humidity

Humidity refers to the amount of moisture in the air. Seed saving is greatly affected by humidity since it affects seed storage conditions, causing them to either become too moist or too dry. The ideal seed storage humidity ranges between 30% and 50%. Too much humidity can lead to seed rot, while too little humidity can cause the seed to dry out. High humidity also promotes the growth of mold and fungi, which can destroy seeds.

Wind

Wind can be both beneficial and detrimental to seed saving. Pollination of crops is often done by wind, which helps to maintain genetic diversity. It also helps to spread seeds to new locations, which helps to maintain genetic diversity and promote the growth of new crops. However, strong winds can also damage plants and dislodge seeds, causing them to be lost. It is important to consider this when selecting a location to save seeds.

Solar Radiation

The amount of sunlight that a plant receives daily significantly affects its growth, development, and seed production. Different plant species have different photoperiod requirements, which refer to the number of hours of daylight or darkness they need to grow and develop. For example, some plants need longer daylight to flower or produce seeds. It is essential to understand the photoperiod requirements of the specific plants you want to save seeds from, to ensure that they receive adequate sunlight to produce viable seeds.

Adapting to Climate Change

One of the most significant challenges that gardeners, farmers, and environmentalists face is adapting to climate change. Climate change is increasingly affecting seed-saving practices as plants' natural habitats are changing due to the changing climatic conditions. One of the significant challenges to seed saving is how to maintain the genetic diversity of plant species that are threatened by climate change. To adapt to the changing climate, it is essential to develop new seed varieties that are more resilient and adaptable to the changing climatic conditions.

To adapt to climate change, seed savers must select plants that are better adapted to current or expected future climatic conditions. This includes selecting varieties that are tolerant to high temperatures, droughts, or extreme weather events such as floods, hurricanes or tornadoes. Additionally, seed savers should consider planting earlier in the growing season, as minimum temperatures are expected to increase.

Conservation of Genetic Diversity

The conservation of genetic diversity should also be a key consideration when saving seeds. Genetic diversity is essential for sustaining plant populations and promoting healthy ecosystems. Genetic diversity provides resilient to stresses such as diseases or pests, and changing climatic conditions. By preserving genetic diversity, seed savers help to maintain healthy ecosystems and preserve the endangered plant species for future generations.

Conclusion

Saving seeds is a critically important practice for promoting biodiversity, conservation of genetic diversity, and adapting to climate change. Climate considerations, such as temperature, rainfall, humidity, wind, and solar radiation, are important when saving seeds. Seed savers must consider how to maintain genetic diversity, conserve plant populations, and adapt to changing climatic conditions. By following the steps outlined in this chapter and working collaboratively, seed savers can help preserve a valuable resource for future generations.

Chapter 47: Seed Saving in Urban Environments

Urban environments are rapidly expanding around the world. With this population shift, there is an increasing need to connect people with their food sources and foster food security. Seed saving is an age-old technique that has been utilized by cultivators for thousands of years. It involves setting aside seeds from a current crop for future planting. Seed saving can reduce a person's reliance on the industrial food system while promoting biodiversity, resilience, and food sovereignty. In this chapter, we delve into how to save seeds in urban areas and why it is vital for communities to engage in this practice.

Why Seed Saving is Important

The food system today is dominated by industrial agriculture, which relies primarily on genetically modified crops that are bred for commercial viability. The result of this is a lack of diversity in the food system. By selecting and saving seeds from the best fruits and vegetables, people can create a diverse and resilient system that can accommodate various environmental and social stresses.

In addition, seed saving can also contribute to food sovereignty. It is the right of people to determine the type of food they consume and how it is grown. By developing and maintaining a collection of regionally adapted, open-pollinated plant varieties, people can sustain food systems that serve their needs.

Seed saving also helps preserve plant diversity. Commercially available seeds usually prioritize profitability, climate resilience, and long shelf-life. Seed libraries, community seed exchanges, and seed-saving initiatives foster plant diversity by preserving and passing on heirloom or rare plant varieties that may be at risk of disappearing.

When creating seed saving initiatives, urban farmers can partner with native plant enthusiasts to increase plant diversity in city gardens. This diversity can increase the value of urban habitats for pollinators, reduce the need for fertilizers, and enhance soil fertility. Pollination by bees, butterflies, and other insects is vital to the success of plants. Many crops would not thrive without the role that pollinators play. By increasing plant diversity and encouraging pollinator habitats, urban gardeners can help support the pollinators living in their areas.

Types of Seeds to Save
When saving seeds, it is vital to remember that not all seeds are created equal. There are three main types of seeds: hybrid, open-pollinated, and heirloom.

Hybrid seeds are the result of two different plant varieties being crossed. The resulting plant is usually stronger, more resistant to disease and pests, and has higher yields. However, unlike open-pollinated and heirloom seeds, hybrid seeds cannot reproduce true to their parent. That means that seeds from hybrid plants will not grow into the same plant as the parent, and future cross-breeding of hybrid plants will produce unpredictable offspring.

Open-pollinated and heirloom seeds, on the other hand, reproduce true to their parents. Open-pollinated seeds are developed without human intervention and are pollinated by wind or insects. Heirloom seeds have a story attached to them and have been passed down for generations. They are usually open-pollinated and have been kept alive by people who value their unique characteristics.

In urban environments, it is best to focus on seed saving initiatives that prioritize open-pollinated and heirloom seeds. These seeds will produce reliable plants, and the seeds can be saved and shared, contributing to a more diverse and resilient food system.

Tips for Seed Saving
Seed saving follows the principle of "plant to seed to plant." Follow these steps to start saving seeds for future planting:

1. Initiate Seed Saving Early
Seed saving can be accomplished early in the growing season. Look for plants that exhibit genetic sustainability and productivity. This means observing the growth characteristics and output of the plant. The fruits, vegetables, or flowers should grow robustly, with fewer pests or diseases compared to other plants.

2. Pick Appropriate Seeds
As mentioned earlier, pick open-pollinated or heirloom seeds to

save. Hybrid seeds are less likely to be productive and will not grow the same plant as the parent.

3. Know Your Plant's Reproduction Method

It is essential to know how your plant reproduces. Some plants are self-pollinating, while others need cross-pollination. By understanding the method, you can ensure that you are correctly collecting the seeds and maintaining the purity of the plant species.

4. Collect Seeds at The Right Time

For seed saving to be successful, you need to collect the seeds at the right time. This means giving the fruit or vegetable time to ripen fully before collecting the seeds. Some fruits or vegetables, such as squash or tomatoes, require you to extract the seeds and dry them before planting.

5. Store Seeds Correctly

Once the seeds are collected, they need to be stored correctly. Consider insect and moisture prevention techniques. Use glass jars or containers that discourage mold from growing. Label the seeds appropriately, including notes on when they were collected and how long they can last.

Urban environments present unique challenges when it comes to seed saving. However, these environments also offer the opportunity to foster food security, promote plant diversity, and support pollinator habitats. By following the principles highlighted in this chapter, urban farmers can join the local food movement, sustain their food supply, and ensure the long-term health of their communities.

Chapter 48: Involving Children in Seed Saving

Saving seeds is a time-honored tradition that has been practiced for generations. Seed saving is the practice of harvesting and storing seeds from plants in order to replant them the following season. This practice is more than just a way to save money on seeds; it is also a way to preserve biodiversity and protect against plant extinction. It is a way to ensure that our favorite varieties of plants and vegetables continue to exist for future generations.

Involving children in seed saving is a wonderful way to instill a love of gardening and an appreciation for the natural world. Children are naturally curious and eager to learn, and incorporating seed saving into their gardening experience can be a fun and educational way to teach them about plant biology and the importance of cultivating and preserving plant species.

There are many benefits to involving children in seed saving:

1. Education: Seed saving provides an opportunity for children to learn about plant biology, the life cycle of plants, pollination, and plant reproduction.

2. Encourages Responsibility: Children take a sense of ownership in their work when they are involved in seed saving. They learn to take responsibility for their plants, nurturing them from seed to harvest.

3. Promotes Sustainability: Seed saving is an eco-friendly practice that reduces waste, preserves biodiversity, and promotes sustainability.

4. Cultures Patience and discipline: Seed saving teaches patience and discipline, as it requires careful attention to timing, proper storage, and handling.

5. Encourages Creativity: Seed saving is an opportunity for children to experiment and create new plant varieties.

Here's how to involve children in seed saving:

1. Start with simple plants – Children need to start working with plants that are easy to grow and easy to save seed from. Examples are sunflowers, marigolds, beans and peas.

2. Get the right equipment – Seed saving requires certain equipment, such as clean containers, scissors, and labels. Involve children in the process of gathering supplies, and explain the importance of having everything in order to be successful.

3. Teach them about plants – Children need to learn about the plants they are growing. Teach them about the different stages of plant growth, and how to tell when the plant is ready for seed harvest.

4. Teach them to recognize and collect seeds from plants – Children

need to learn about seed morphology; for example, some seeds have an outer covering, or hull, that needs to be removed. They must be able to identify mature fruit that contains seed; for example, tomato seeds will be harvested from mature red tomatoes. Talk to them about the pros and cons of harvesting seeds from hybrid or regionally adapted varieties.

5. Create a seed notebook – Encourage children to create a seed notebook where they can make notes on the planting, growth, and harvesting of the plants, and include pictures of the plants and seeds. This will also help them keep track of which seeds they have already saved.

6. Properly store saved seeds – It is important that seeds are properly stored to ensure they remain viable. Teach children that seeds need to be dried thoroughly before storing them, and stored in a cool, dry, and dark place. Ensure that they learn how to label the containers and how to record each essential detail, such as the variety, year saved, etc.

7. Encourage experimentation – Seed saving also gives children the opportunity to experiment and create new plant varieties. Encourage them to cross-pollinate plants and see what kind of new varieties they can come up with.

Seed saving can be a fun and educational practice that instills a sense of responsibility for caring for the earth. By involving children in this activity, we can help them develop a lifelong love of gardening, and a respect for the natural world.

Involving children in seed saving is a wonderful way to promote an appreciation for the natural world, and to teach children about the importance of cultivating and preserving plant species. Through seed saving, children can learn to take responsibility for their plants, experiment and create new plant varieties, and develop skills that will enable them to care for the environment for years to come.

Chapter 49: Incorporating Seed Saving in Education

The concept of seed saving is as ancient as farming itself. It is the art of collecting and preserving seeds from plants for future use. In recent times, there has been a growing awareness of the importance of seed saving, especially in our modern era, where industrial agriculture has dominated the market, and genetic diversity in our food systems is threatened. Incorporating seed saving in education is a vital component in ensuring the preservation of plant biodiversity and empowering students with the knowledge to sustainably produce food.

Seed Saving: An Overview:
Seed saving is the process of collecting and preserving seeds from plants that one intends to grow in the future. The process involves selecting healthy plants with desirable characteristics and allowing them to produce mature seeds. The seeds are then collected and dried before being stored in a safe and dry place. In this manner, seed savers can maintain and pass on the genetic diversity of plants. Instead of relying on industrial agriculture, individuals can grow their foods, select seeds that are adapted to their local conditions, and save seeds for future harvests.

Why Incorporate Seed Saving in Education?
Incorporating seed saving in education is essential in a time when our food systems are under threat. On the one hand, many plant species have become extinct, and others are at risk of disappearing.

This loss threatens biodiversity and impacts the availability of nutritious foods. Traditional seed-saving has the potential to help ensure survival despite changing climate conditions and other challenges faced by our modern food production system. Providing students with the skill to save seeds will empower them to adapt their farming practices to fit local climatic conditions. They'll also be able to modify their crops according to their own needs and those of their community.

Incorporating seed saving into the curriculum also helps young people develop an appreciation for plant biodiversity, food sovereignty and the need to protect and conserve crops. They will learn about the cultural significance of different crops and the importance of preserving the heritage of their communities. As they grow to appreciate the significance of these heritage plants, their concern for their conservation will grow. They'll be inspired to grow and propagate them through traditional seed-saving, knowing that they're a part of something much larger.

Moreover, seed saving will expose young people to fundamental scientific principles. They will learn about the biology of plants, genetics, ecology, and microorganisms. Students will be introduced to holistic thinking about ecosystems and how different biological systems interact to contribute to a sustainable agricultural system.

How to Incorporate Seed Saving in Education
Incorporating seed saving in the curriculum is relatively

straightforward. Below are some ways in which teachers can engage their students in the seed-saving process.

1. Plant a school garden: Growing a school garden is an excellent way to introduce seed saving in education. The garden can act as a living classroom where students can learn about the life cycles of plants, the uses of different crops, and the importance of biodiversity. The school garden can also serve as a platform for growing heritage crops, which are then used for seed saving.

2. Invite guest speakers: Teachers can invite guest speakers such as seed savers, farmers, and gardening experts, to educate students on the importance of seed saving and the role it plays in food production. Guest speakers can explain the intricacies of seed saving, provide practical skills, and share their experiences.

3. Field trips: Teachers can take students on field trips to farms, seed banks, and botanical gardens that have seed-saving programs. This will provide students with a practical experience and exposure to different seed-saving techniques.

4. Seed saving workshops: Teachers can organize seed saving workshops within the classroom or at the school garden. These workshops can provide practical training on seed-saving techniques such as seed harvesting, processing, storage, and methods of germination.

5. Heritage seed library: Teachers can establish a seed library at school to create a self-sustaining seed-saving program. Students can exchange saved seeds, creating a learning community focused on traditional seed-saving and enriching the school grounds with diverse plants.

Incorporating seed saving in education is an effective way to ensure students understand the importance of preserving biodiversity in agriculture ultimately. It provides an opportunity to engage students in practical learning while having a lasting impact on their lives. Through seed saving, students gain necessary knowledge and practical skills to adapt to changing conditions, promote food sovereignty, and above all contribute to the development and conservation of their communities.

Chapter 50: Future of Seed Saving

For thousands of years, farmers and gardeners have been saving seeds from their crops to plant the following year, creating a cycle of seed selection and breeding that has resulted in the incredible diversity of plants that we enjoy today. However, with the rise of industrial agriculture and genetically modified crops, the practice of seed saving has become less common. Many farmers are now reliant on patented seeds from large corporations, and the biodiversity of our food system is at risk.

But there is hope. A growing number of farmers, gardeners, and seed enthusiasts are working to preserve traditional seed varieties and promote seed saving as a way to ensure food security for future generations. In this chapter, we will explore the history of seed saving, the challenges facing seed savers today, and the exciting opportunities for the future of seed saving.

History of Seed Saving

The practice of saving seeds dates back to the dawn of agriculture. Early farmers selected and saved the seeds from their best-performing crops, gradually improving the quality and yield of their harvests. Over time, this led to the development of diverse crops that were adapted to local climates and growing conditions.

In the 20th century, the rise of industrial agriculture and the use of hybrid seeds changed the way seeds were produced and distributed. Hybrid seeds, which are created by crossing two different varieties of plants, provide consistent yields and disease resistance, but cannot be saved from year to year. Instead, farmers are required to purchase new seeds each year from seed companies.

At the same time, the consolidation of seed companies and the rise of genetically modified crops have led to a decline in seed diversity. Large corporations now control the majority of the global seed market, and many traditional seed varieties have been lost or are in danger of disappearing.

The Challenges Facing Seed Savers

Despite the importance of seed saving for preserving biodiversity and ensuring food security, there are several challenges facing seed savers today.

One of the biggest challenges is the legal framework surrounding seed saving. Many seeds are now patented by large corporations, which means that farmers are not allowed to save and replant them without permission. This has created a situation where farmers are reliant on a small number of companies for their seed supply, which can be expensive and limiting.

Another challenge is the loss of traditional knowledge around seed saving. Many younger farmers and gardeners have not grown up with the practice of seed saving, and may not know how to properly save and store seeds for future use. This has led to a decline in seed diversity, as less common varieties are not being propagated and preserved.

Finally, climate change presents a major challenge for seed savers. As temperatures and weather patterns shift, crops may no longer be adapted to the local climate, and new varieties may need to be developed to ensure food security. This requires a strong seed saving community and the ability to quickly adapt and breed new varieties of crops.

The Future of Seed Saving

Despite these challenges, there are many exciting opportunities for the future of seed saving.

One of the most promising developments is the rise of community seed banks and seed libraries. These organizations allow individuals to borrow and donate seeds, creating a network of local seed sources that can be adapted to local growing conditions. Seed banks also provide a way to preserve rare and unusual varieties of crops that might otherwise be lost.

In addition, there are a growing number of organizations dedicated to promoting seed saving and protecting seed diversity. These groups work to educate farmers and gardeners about seed saving techniques, and advocate for policies that support seed diversity and independence.

Finally, advances in technology are making it easier to breed and develop new crop varieties. Tools like CRISPR-Cas9 gene editing allow scientists to make precise changes to plant DNA, which could lead to the development of crops that are more disease-resistant, drought-tolerant, or adapted to changing climates.

Seed saving is a critical component of a healthy and sustainable food system. While there are many challenges facing seed savers today, there are also exciting opportunities for the future of seed saving. By working together to preserve and protect our seed diversity, we can ensure that future generations have access to a wide variety of nutritious and delicious crops.

www.ingramcontent.com/pod-product-compliance
Lightning Source LLC
Chambersburg PA
CBHW051506030726
47592CB00006B/2125